D1567509

Edward Larrabee Barnes

Edward Larrabee Barnes

EDWARD LARRABEE BARNES ARCHITECT

Introduction by Peter Blake

RIZZOLI
NEW YORK

Special Thanks

Several people made this book what it is: my friend
Massimo Vignelli, who did the clear, bold design;
Genie Devine, who carefully coordinated every detail;
Abigail Sturges, who painstakingly executed the design;
and David Morton and Andrea Monfried,
who edited the book. They have my appreciation,
admiration, and affection.

Edward Larrabee Barnes

First published in the United States of America in 1994 by
Rizzoli International Publications, Inc.
300 Park Avenue South, New York, New York 10010

Library of Congress Cataloging-in-Publication Data
Edward Larrabee Barnes, architect / introduction by Peter Blake.
p. cm.
ISBN 0-8478-1821-7 (hardcover). — ISBN 0-8478-1822-5 (paperback).
1. Barnes, Edward Larrabee, 1915– . I. Barnes, Edward Larrabee, 1915– .
NA737.B27E35 1994   94-14244
720'.92—dc20   CIP

Front cover illustration:
599 Lexington Avenue, New York, New York, 1981–1986
Back cover illustration:
Heckscher House, Mount Desert Island, Maine, 1971–1974

Design: Massimo Vignelli
Design Coordinator: Abigail Sturges

Printed and bound in Singapore

Contents

Acknowledgments

This year, with mixed feelings, I am giving up my office practice to become a consultant. This book looks back on a happy professional life of forty-five years.

The task of condensing such a career into one volume has not been easy. Some of my favorite clients and buildings have been relegated to the Chronology, and many of my past associates are barely mentioned. I can only hope that old friends will know how much they have meant to me.

I am deeply indebted to my current associates—Dan Casey, Gajinder Singh, and Steve Fisher—and to my partners—John Lee for his perceptive intelligence and strong design, Percy Keck for his unfailing integrity in architecture and office management, and Alistair Bevington for his hands-on artistry.

Finally, there is Mary, whose sure eye, color sense, understanding of people, architectural sensitivity, and total unselfishness have underpinned all of my work.

Edward Larrabee Barnes
May 1994

Introduction

In the late 1930s and early 1940s, when most schools of architecture in the United States were still dominated by the beaux-arts system, the Harvard Graduate School of Design was an extraordinary exception: under the leadership of Dean Joseph Hudnut, Harvard had hired Walter Gropius and Marcel Breuer—formerly of the Bauhaus in pre-Nazi Germany—and several others of similar aesthetic persuasion to teach a new generation of idealistic young architects. Over a very brief period of time, these teachers inspired a truly remarkable group of students whose names are now synonymous with the modern movement in America: Henry Cobb, Ulrich Franzen, John Harkness, John Johansen, Philip Johnson, I. M. Pei, Paul Rudolph, and many, many more.

Edward Larrabee Barnes was one of that group whose members went on to design and build much of what is best on the new American skyline. Barnes, perhaps more than his contemporaries, remained faithful to the original vision while thoughtfully adapting it to the American situation.

This book is, of course, primarily devoted to Barnes's impressive buildings; but it is also devoted to his very special notion of how modernism could most effectively accommodate the opportunities and contradictions of the postwar world.

While many of his classmates are best known for their personal signatures, Barnes will be remembered for a more selfless contribution. In almost all of his buildings he responds to the situations in which he finds himself. He seems to have grasped what few others understood as clearly and as creatively—that a designed building, in a participatory democracy, should respond to a great variety of factors and that its ultimate form should express those conditions and demands rather than provide a memorial to its architect or to those who paid the bill.

Such factors comprise the site, including the nature of the neighborhood; the function that the building will accommodate; the special needs and preferences of the clients and ultimate users of the building; the budget; the various regulations and limitations imposed by local authorities; the image that the building is to project; the appropriate structural or mechanical systems to serve all of the above; the climate; and much more.

Then, of course, there is the matter of art. For the architect's most important function, in the end, is to resolve all of the factors, to determine how much weight each commands, and to translate all of this into a single, unified work of art. That work will, in turn, reflect personal experiences and preferences, memories of things past, and dreams of things to come.

Translating these often contradictory factors into a unified, organic work of architecture seems incredibly difficult—and it is. In prepopulist times, this was much less of a problem than it has been since architecture became a highly visible aspect of a multifaceted, democratic society. At a time when the function of architecture was primarily to memorialize popes and princes and other power brokers, most of the above factors were easily resolved: the building had merely to dominate its site; its function was to glorify. As for cost, image, local regulations, etc.—who remembers what the Parthenon cost? Who wrote the building code for Chartres Cathedral?

The overriding problem for architects in the past was how to make a monument that was also art. If the pope or prince was sophisticated enough to hire Michelangelo or Borromini, the resulting building would very probably end up in the history books.

Clearly the forces that shape architecture today, and that have shaped our buildings ever since the advent of democracy, changed all of the rules. The situation is vastly more complex than when the Parthenon and Chartres were built. Some very serious and very thoughtful architects have responded to these dramatic changes by suggesting that some sort of colorful "pop" chaos might be an appropriate response to the seemingly chaotic situation created by the growth of participatory democracy.

It is an interesting idea but suggests an abdication of responsibility. After all, if chaos is the appropriate image of our time, then why pursue the art of architecture at all?

To most of those who belonged to Barnes's generation,

this abdication of responsibility was, quite simply, silly—or worse, an exercise in condescension. To Barnes and his contemporaries, the objective of architecture was and is to set certain examples of excellence, in form as well as function, that generate an equally civilized response. They did not lay down the law for their fellow men and women, imposing a set of rules by which people must live. Instead, they spent a great deal of energy responding to the varied demands of a complex society in ways that enhance the quality of life.

Ed Barnes was born in Chicago in 1915, into a well-to-do family of professionals and artists. His father, Cecil Barnes, a lawyer, graduated from Harvard; his mother, the writer Margaret Ayer Barnes, successfully dramatized Edith Wharton's *Age of Innocence* on Broadway in 1928 and in 1931 won a Pulitzer Prize for her novel *Years of Grace*. As an undergraduate at Harvard, Barnes first majored in English. He later switched to art history, and then to the history of architecture.

After graduation, he decided to spend a year teaching at Milton Academy, his old preparatory school outside Boston. There, in addition to English literature, he taught classes in art and architecture. It was in the course of preparing a series of architectural lectures that he visited the houses that Walter Gropius and Marcel Breuer had built for themselves and their families in nearby Lincoln. "I went there hoping to borrow scale models of their houses to show my students," Barnes recalls, "but when I saw Breuer's house—when I was actually *in* it—I decided that this was what I wanted to be: an architect."

The Gropius and Breuer houses were exciting and radical in the eyes of Barnes's students and in his eyes as well: flat-roofed, glass-walled, cantilevered. Barnes, whose politics were, in any case, left-wing, thought that this daring new architecture was just the thing for him. And so he returned to Harvard, this time to the Harvard Graduate School of Design.

Although Gropius ran the school, commanding admiration and respect, Breuer seems to have been most effective in shaping Barnes and his fellow students. Gropius was a logical and persuasive theorist; Breuer was primarily an artist who conveyed his ideas poetically, in close personal relationships with his students. Hungarian by birth and hampered by imperfect English, Breuer communicated through drawings and models of projects addressed in the design studio. To this day, years after his death, Breuer's students remember him with affection and gratitude—although many of them have gone off in directions of which their former teacher might not entirely approve.

Right after graduating from architecture school, Barnes received a Sheldon Traveling Fellowship. Travel was limited because of the war in Europe, and Barnes spent his fellowship year in Washington as an intern at the Division of Defense Housing. After the Pearl Harbor bombing, he joined the Naval Reserve as an architect at Hunter's Point, San Francisco. Following the war and a brief period working for the architect Bill Wurster in San Francisco, Barnes took a job with the industrial designer Henry Dreyfuss in Los Angeles. Dreyfuss had been asked by Consolidated Vultee, a manufacturer of military aircraft during World War II, to design a mass-producible, single-family house that would help the company convert its facilities to peacetime production; and Gropius had advised Dreyfuss to hire Barnes as architect.

The house was never mass-produced, but a number of prototypes were manufactured and tested. They were very high-tech for their day—and seem quite advanced fifty years later: the walls, where not floor-to-ceiling glass, were extremely thin aluminum-faced, paper honeycomb core panels; the detailing was precise, elegant, and neat. Alas, problems of distribution and union opposition, plus the withdrawal of government funding, ultimately killed the project, but it reminds us of the dedicated spirit and the preoccupation with housing of young architects in the postwar period. As Barnes says today, "At that time there was no question in my mind that modern architecture and social commitment were inextricably linked." Barnes did other low-cost housing projects after World War II, notably El Monte in San Juan, Puerto Rico, and Capitol Towers in Sacramento, but the economic and political climate was changing and architects were no longer involved in the one area about which many of them felt most passionately.

After the stint in the Dreyfuss office, Barnes returned east with his wife, Mary, and settled in New York, where he opened his own office. The couple lived in a typically avant-garde Manhattan apartment: to keep the place flawlessly neat, visitors were asked to trade in their shoes for Japanese paper slippers at the entrance.

Barnes's design work was just as neat. In subtle ways, however, it was rather different from the work of his Harvard mentors. An early house, for Robert and Elodie Osborn, in Salisbury, Connecticut (1949–1950), was remarkable in several respects, including its maturity. Its most obvious "non-modern" aspect was the symmetry of its plan and elevations. Symmetry had been a no-no among modern architects like Breuer: it seemed to hark back to an earlier time, when architecture was an elitist pursuit and the prince or pope who commissioned a particular monument was placed at the center of a balanced composition. Yet Barnes saw nothing wrong with symmetry per se—if the building requirements seemed to suggest it. Already in this delightful little white-walled, flat-roofed platform house, he revealed a pragmatic independence that would later serve him exceedingly well. And as his practice grew to include large-scale works—art museums, whole college campuses, and skyscrapers—his responses became increasingly varied.

While some of his contemporaries were developing signature styles, so that their own, unmistakable imprint dominated everything else, each of Barnes's buildings responded to many factors, not the least of which was his constant absorption of ideas and images from the past and the present as he traveled around the world—and used his eyes.

Like other architects with sizable practices, Barnes has worked with a large number of collaborators. But unlike most architects of his generation, he seems to have launched a whole new group of independent practitioners who received some of their "basic training" in his office. Literally hundreds of young men and women, from many different parts of the world, have passed through the Barnes office. Many contributed considerably to Barnes's projects before starting their own practices—often with significant and generous assistance from their former employer, who would steer potential clients to them.

His most important collaborator over the years has been his wife, Mary. Mary Cooke began her career in London, where she studied at the Architectural Association. After seeing Tecton's Penguin Pool in 1934, she went to work for that office, a group of seven architects united by their interest in good design and social commitment.

Back in the United States in 1937, Mary organized a show at the Museum of Modern Art on Alvar Aalto, and soon after went to Washington to work in public housing. Then, in 1943, the U.S. Office of War Information and MoMA collaborated on an exhibition, "American Housing in War and Peace, 1918–1944," with Catherine Bauer as the consultant and Mary as the designer. The show opened in London and traveled in Europe. After the war, when the Barneses came back to New York from California, Mary served as curator of architecture at MoMA from 1947 to 1949.

In 1950 her life changed. She combined motherhood with work in the Barnes office. There she worked on every kind of job, including the selection and commissioning of works of art. Needless to say, her museum experience was a great asset.

Mary was and is an astute in-house critic, and her importance to the development of her husband's practice has been considerable. The complex relationships in any professional office require not only a high level of perceptiveness but a high degree of tact. She possesses both.

Barnes's strength is his ability to relate and adjust to all of the different conditions that determine the ultimate shape of a work of architecture. He is an extremely sophisticated artist, fully aware of the many options open to a twentieth-century architect and familiar with the directions explored by his generation and by earlier pioneers.

In his work, the plans are direct and simple. There is

a central rational idea or theme. Yet this doesn't mean that he is simplistic, or has a formula, or designs dominant signature buildings. On the contrary, he is extremely responsive to the variety implicit in a multifaceted society, to the contextual implications of urban and natural settings, and to the unique demands of each new problem. His work has clarity and at the same time respects the complexity and variety of modern life.

Three very different projects demonstrate Barnes's extraordinary sensitivity to the special conditions presented by each: Haystack Mountain School of Crafts in Maine (1958–1961); the forty-story office building for the New England Merchants National Bank in Boston (1963–1970); and the Thurgood Marshall Federal Judiciary Building in Washington, D.C. (1988–1992). No three buildings constructed over this thirty-year period in the United States—or, possibly, anywhere else—could be more different; and few observers would guess that they had been designed by the same architect.

Yet all three projects reveal the remarkable sensitivity and special talent that makes Barnes's work unique. These buildings reflect and respond to very special conditions:

• Haystack, on Deer Isle in Maine, is not a building but a village of shingled cottages linked by a grid of walkways or wooden decks that lead to a spectacular view of the ocean. It is one of the most beautiful places imaginable for a summer spent learning a craft. The architecture critic Robert Campbell, writing about Haystack twenty-five years after it was built, said that its "simplicity, its natural materials, its clean-cut angular shapes, its vernacular reference, its attitude of leaving nature untouched—all those qualities exercised an influence that was immediate and strong, but remains largely unrecognized. A whole generation of shed-roofed American buildings . . . belongs in some degree to a tradition begun by Ed Barnes at Haystack Mountain."

• The New England Merchants National Bank building that Barnes designed half a dozen years later for the new City Hall Plaza in Boston stands next to the Old State House and the sixteen-story Ames Building of

1882–1885 by H. H. Richardson. Right around the corner is Faneuil Hall; not much farther off is the restored Quincy Market area. The city hall and various equally "brutalist," exposed concrete structures are also within sight. To design a building that would relate to all of these and serve not only its users and neighbors but pedestrians approaching the plaza—this seems enough to challenge the most talented architect.

Barnes met the challenge in a gentle, understated fashion, with a building that creates spaces and walkways around its base, unlike many of its neighbors. The building is really a series of pedestrian links, all of them thoughtfully considered, all of them pleasant, all of them helpful. The skin of the building is red-gray granite—a kind of gray flannel suit—very Bostonian, very understated, very elegant. It looks considerably better today than most of its contemporary neighbors. Like Haystack, it has stood the test of time.

• The judiciary building in Washington, D.C., is located next to Daniel Burnham's 1903–1907 Union Station. Given the city's preoccupation with its past, the client expected (and received) numerous proposals for imitative, neo-neoclassicist designs paying respect to Burnham. Barnes (and his recent partner John M. Y. Lee) did indeed pay their respects—in scale, materials, relationship of windows to walls—but they did so in a truly creative fashion, without aping Burnham's ornate facades. The result is a de Chirico version of a classical piazza—a hard-edged, simplified arcade, designed to frame fragments from a fairly distant past. It is an extraordinarily sensitive and charming response to yet another special situation, and quite different from the responses Barnes offered elsewhere.

And properly so. In each of the examples cited above, the architect made a conscious effort to rethink architecture—to create a synthesis of innumerable forces and factors that are then resolved in a single, convincing work of art. Not many architects in the second half of this century have tackled the problems presented to them quite so selflessly, and with such elegance and art. One senses that the work of Ed Barnes will stand the test of time very gracefully. Indeed, it already has.

Buildings and Projects

Prefabricated House

Consolidated Vultee Aircraft Corporation
1946–1947
Henry Dreyfuss, Designer
Edward Larrabee Barnes, Architect

Bottom: Aluminum-panel corner connection with snap-in cover (paper honeycomb core not shown).

1 Entrance
2 Patio
3 Living room
4 Kitchen
5 Bedroom
6 Service

One forgets that in the 1930s and 1940s, a social conscience was integral to a modern architect's makeup. Aalto, Mies, Gropius, and Breuer, even Wright, did low-cost housing. The Museum of Modern Art sponsored housing shows. Architectural magazines published Clarence Stein, Catherine Bauer, and Lewis Mumford. My 1938 college thesis was a study of a United States Housing Authority housing project. Later, with a Harvard University Sheldon Fellowship, I studied defense housing in Washington and around the country. For me it was a given—social reform and modern architecture were inseparable.

For a little while, right after the war, I actually got a chance to *design* low-cost housing. In 1946 the federal government supported a Guaranteed Market Program to provide affordable housing and jobs for displaced war workers. Henry Dreyfuss, the industrial designer, offered me a job working with him on a prefabricated house for Consolidated Vultee Aircraft.

The house, built in an aircraft factory, was fabricated of lightweight aluminum panels with a paper honeycomb core. Unlike other prefab houses of the time, which were made of small modular panels, ours used full-length wall panels shipped flat to the site. A prototype was built in the factory, and later two- and three-bedroom models were erected, furnished, and occupied. An L-shaped patio wall could be sited to screen the house from the street or from neighbors.

Sadly, after a few years the Guaranteed Market Program was terminated, and across the country prefabrication came to a halt.

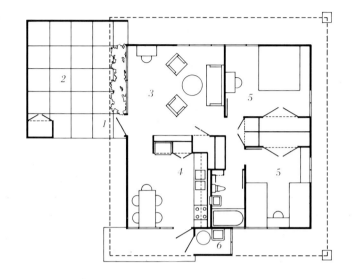

0   5   10   15 ft

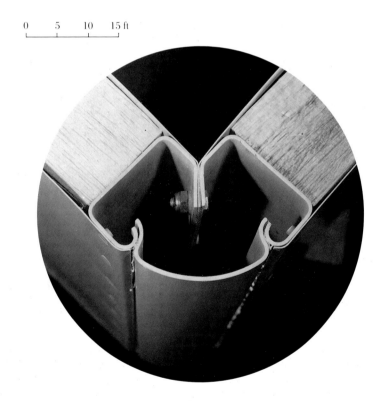

Capitol Towers Apartments

Sacramento, California
1957–1960

El Monte Apartments

San Juan, Puerto Rico
1958–1961, 1967

1 High-rise apartments
2 Garage
3 Low-rise apartments

In the late 1950s Jim Scheuer (later a member of Congress) gave me a chance to work on two low-cost redevelopment projects—one in Sacramento associated with Wurster, Bernardi and Emmons and with DeMars and Reay, and another in San Juan associated with an old friend, Bill Reed of Reed, Basora and Menendez. In the Sacramento Capitol Towers Apartments, I did the low-rise and Wurster's office did the high-rise. My inexpensive two-story, frame and stucco construction has apartments on the first floor opening onto private patios and on the second floor looking out in the other direction over common park space. This reversal of orientation plus the rambling site plan, made possible by open breezeways, is all there is to the design, but the informality has charm.

The El Monte Apartments in San Juan are more ambitious. Serpentine high-rise buildings follow the contours of the site. Ground-floor apartments (with private patios) and top-floor apartments are one-story units. The others are two-story duplexes, really little town houses, with the access corridor *outside*—a continuous, single-loaded open sidewalk. The living room–kitchen floor opens off the corridor and looks out onto a double-height balcony in the back. Above, one bedroom overlooks the entrance canopies along the access corridor and the other looks out over the balcony. All apartments have privacy and cross ventilation. In San Juan, with year-round trade winds, air-conditioning is not needed.

The curse of most large-scale housing project facades is repetitive, low floor heights and small windows. In El Monte the stacked duplexes cut the scale of the fourteen floors in half. The counterpoint of single- and double-height apartments enlivens the facades.

Around the base of the slabs are two- and three-story row houses, informally arranged to follow site contours. Studio apartments with barrel vaults are positioned above certain two-story units.

Site plan, Capitol Towers Apartments

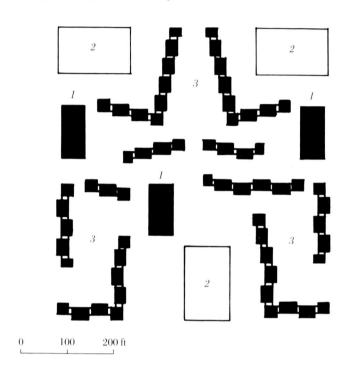

0   100   200 ft

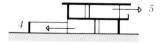

0   20   40 ft

1 Private walled patio
2 Balcony overlooking public space
3 Living room
4 Parking
5 Public space
6 Open breezeway

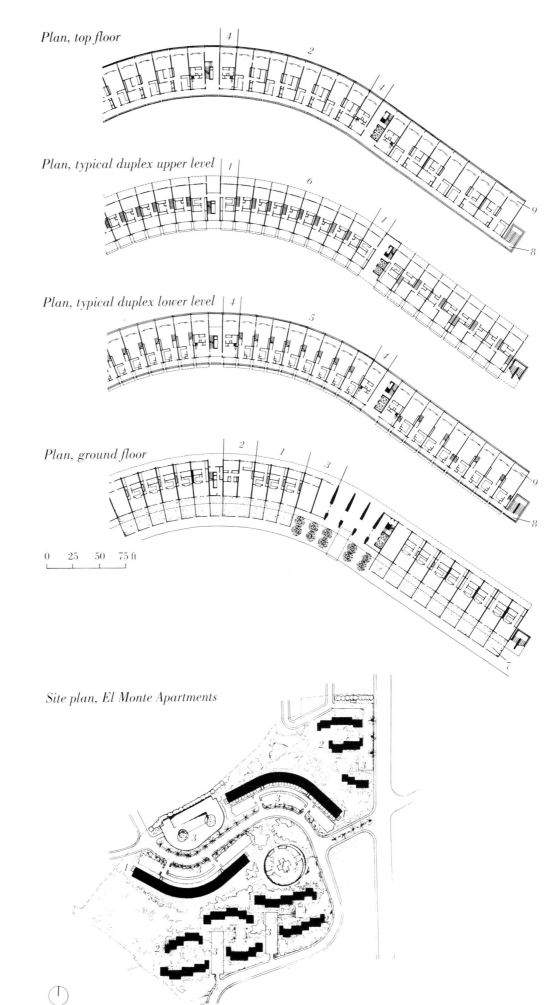

1 One-bedroom apartment
2 Two-bedroom apartment
3 Storage and meeting
  rooms
4 Studio apartment
5 Two-bedroom duplex,
  lower level
6 Two-bedroom duplex,
  upper level
7 Entrance patio
8 Access corridor
9 Balcony

Plan, top floor

Plan, typical duplex upper level

Plan, typical duplex lower level

Plan, ground floor

0   25   50   75 ft

1 High-rise apartments
2 Low-rise apartments
3 Parking
4 Pool

Site plan, El Monte Apartments

Opposite: El Monte high-rise apartments, with exterior corridors and entrance canopies.

Below: El Monte duplex apartment balconies.

Bottom: El Monte row houses with studio apartments above.

Osborn House

Salisbury, Connecticut, 1949–1950

There *is* such a thing as an "architectural" idea, one that derives from function, circulation, and site. In the 1950s I designed several houses raised on platforms in open meadow land: the Barnes, Buck, Marsters, and Osborn houses.

The defined entrance terrace of this house focuses on the front door. A living-dining terrace features formal shade trees, and a private master bedroom terrace frames sculpture against the view (the owners possess a fine collection of sculpture and paintings by Calder, Miró, and Klee). Indoor and outdoor spaces interlock— all on the stone platform. Beyond the platform is farmland with hay blowing in the wind.

Buck House

Barnes House

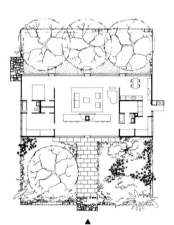

Marsters House

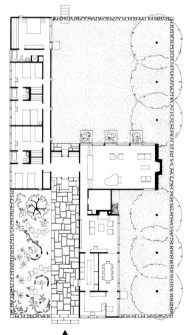

0   20   40 ft

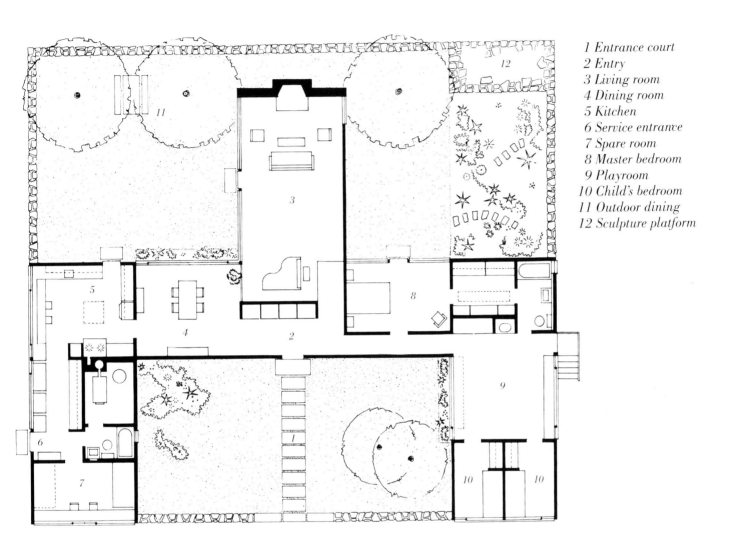

1 Entrance court
2 Entry
3 Living room
4 Dining room
5 Kitchen
6 Service entrance
7 Spare room
8 Master bedroom
9 Playroom
10 Child's bedroom
11 Outdoor dining
12 Sculpture platform

0   5   10   15 ft

Below: Entrance terrace.   *Bottom: Master-bedroom terrace.*

Straus House

Pound Ridge, New York, 1956–1958

This is a family house on a beautiful private lake. I did not want to mar the site with a glaring modern house; instead I used dark brown siding and a black post-and-lintel laminated wood frame. The house floats above the rocky shoreline on columns that hardly disturb the terrain. The screened porch, a separate pavilion, hovers over the lake. The autonomous wings (living, dining, master bedroom, and children) connect via glazed passageways. Only the living-room ceiling rises above the quiet roofline. In the peaks of the roof, as well as under the overhangs between the beams, is dark blue and purple stained glass.

The house mimics primitive Japanese buildings, clearly expressing the post-and-lintel construction. Beams run east and west on a regular module. The roof joists, above the beams, run north and south.

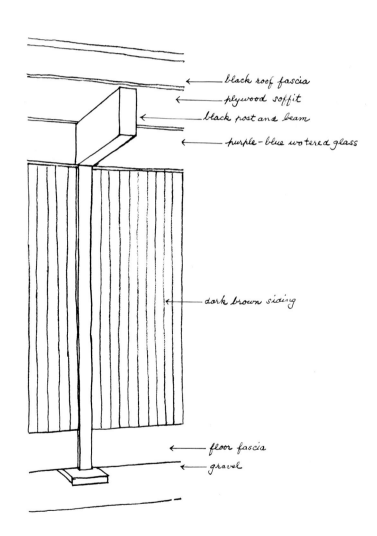

black roof fascia
plywood soffit
black post and beam
purple-blue watered glass

dark brown siding

floor fascia
gravel

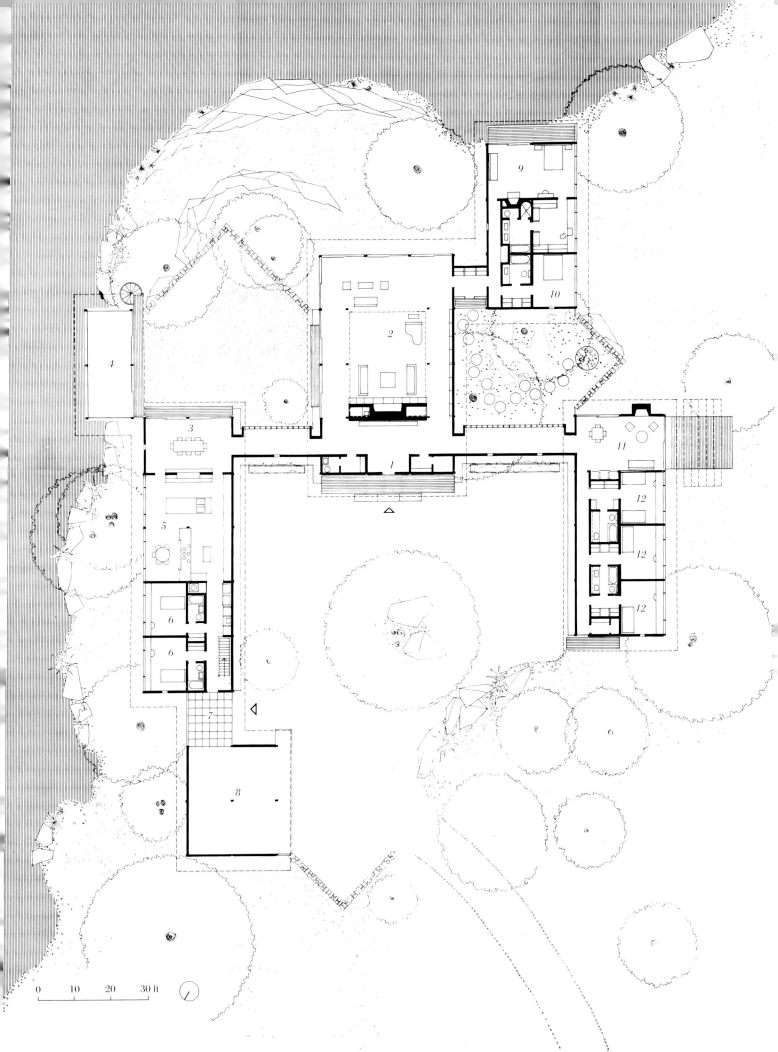

0   10   20   30 ft

Below: Living room with   *Opposite: Screened porch.*
stained glass in roof peak.

Cowles House

Wayzata, Minnesota, 1959–1962

As one comes up the drive, this house looks like a village. One enters a "farm courtyard." Roof peaks rise above major spaces in the primarily single-story structure. White fences, arbors, and low stone walls define paddocks, orchards, and terraces.

The interiors are as continuous as the exterior, with gray-green slate floors and white walls. The gables contain great areas of fixed glass while many of the lower windows and screens disappear into pockets in the wall, leaving large, uncluttered openings.

In 1972 the house was greatly enlarged and turned into a conference center (see Spring Hill Conference Center in the Chronology).

Below: Early sketch of pinwheel plan.

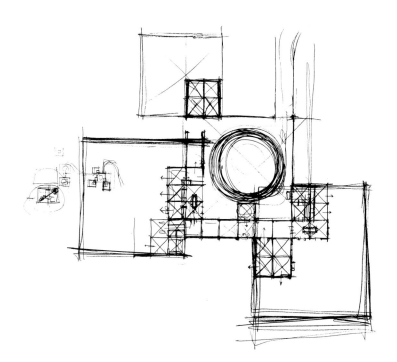

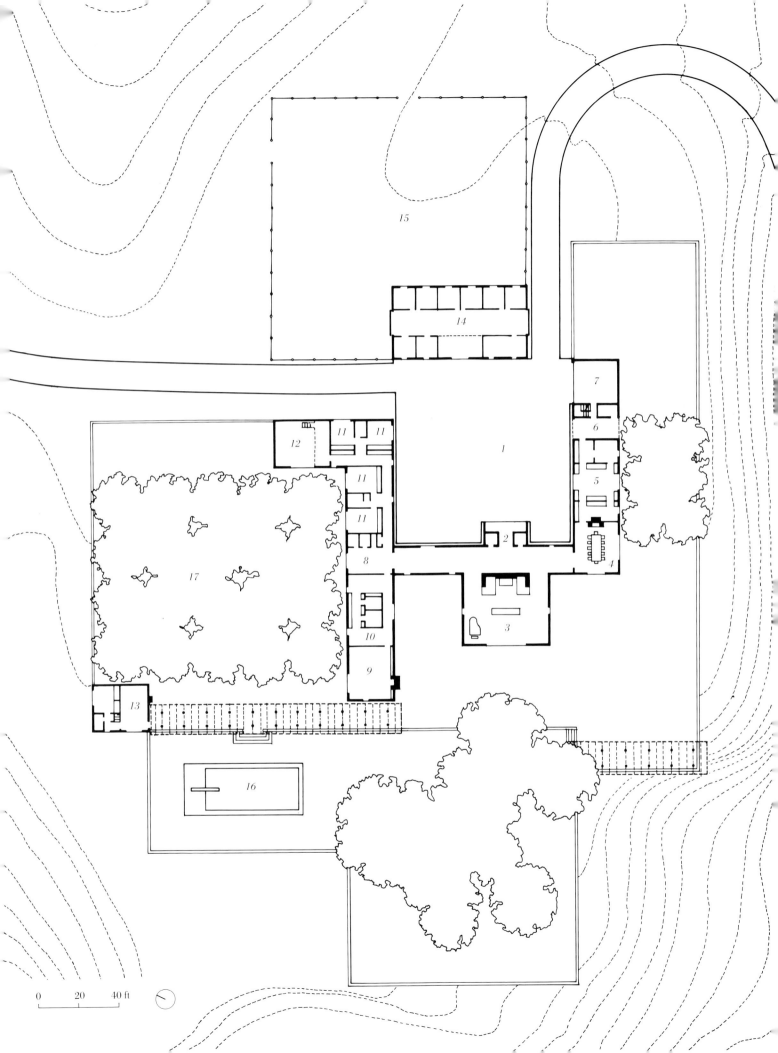

1

2

3

4

5

6

7

8

9

10

11

11

11

11

12

13

14

15

16

17

0   20   40 ft

Opposite: Peaked windows in living room, pocket window in dining room.

Below: The master bedroom is at left; the living room at right.

Bottom: Stable.

Righter House

Fishers Island, New York, 1963–1965

The form of this weekend house for a couple responds to the views: a wide, low glass wall looks out to sea, and a tall, vertical glass wall looks out on a grove of trees. The kitchen–dining room and bedroom balcony above look inland; the living room flares out toward the ocean.

The bold exterior mass contains an interior volume that shifts from low and wide to tall and narrow. The exterior is wood shingled; the interior, natural wood siding.

A separate guest house, garage, and low, shingled wall define the entrance court.

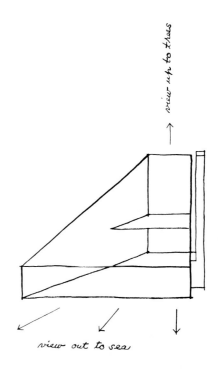

view up to trees

view out to sea

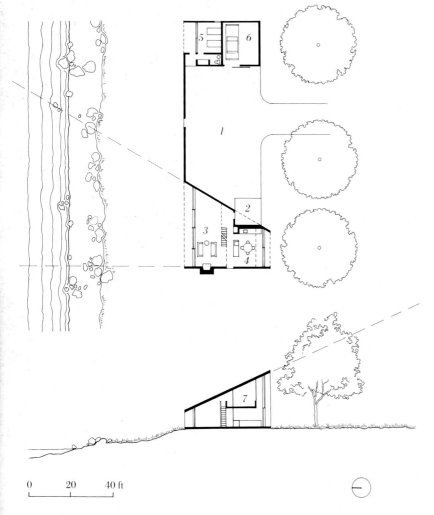

1 *Entrance court*
2 *Entry*
3 *Living room*
4 *Kitchen–dining room*
5 *Guest house*
6 *Garage*
7 *Master bedroom and bath*

0   20   40 ft

Heckscher House

Mount Desert Island, Maine, 1971–1974

This is a house for private lives and family gatherings. The man is a scholar-author; the woman is interested in art, calligraphy, and cooking. The children are independent, well past college age. Friends come for long visits.

The house consists of four buildings: a studio tower with laundry below; a one-bedroom main house with a living room, dining room, and kitchen; a two-story guest house; and a high-ceilinged library. A meandering wood deck that widens into separate verandas unifies the whole. It is like a Maine fishing village for one family.

A simple enclosing form, roofs and walls in one material, covers the interior volumes. Note the shingled corner where wall and roof planes meet.

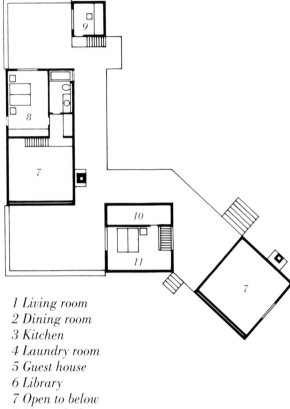

Plan, upper floor

1 Living room
2 Dining room
3 Kitchen
4 Laundry room
5 Guest house
6 Library
7 Open to below
8 Master bedroom
9 Studio
10 Storage
11 Guest bedroom

Plan, ground floor

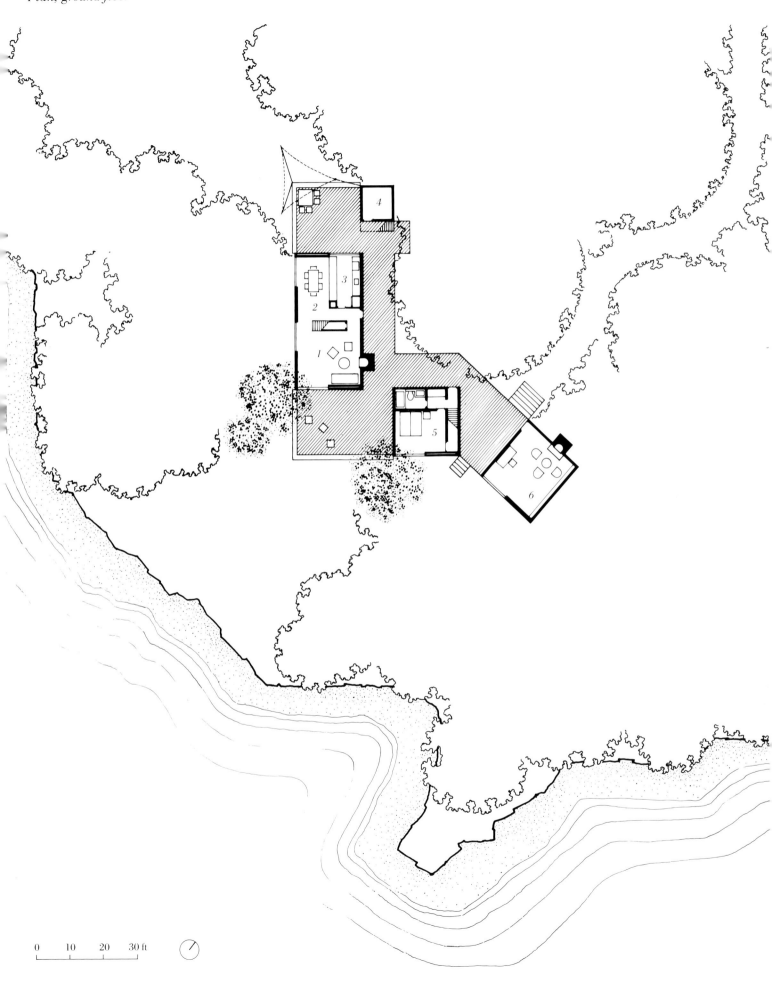

0   10   20   30 ft

Below: Guest house.

Bottom: Library.

Opposite: Guest house with
library beyond.

Below: Volumetric architecture—the shingled planes meet without an overhang.

Opposite: Living room with studio tower beyond.

Below: Living room, dining room, and bedroom balcony in main house.

Opposite: Dining veranda, kitchen, and studio tower.

House in Dallas, Texas

1980–1983

Overleaf: Entrance court.

This house steps downhill from the street into a ravine. Designed for a family with older children, the bedrooms are separated—the master bedroom in one wing, the girls' rooms on two floors in another, and the boy's quarters in an apartment over the garage. From the street the house looks like separate blocks linked only by breezeways—or "dog runs," in Texas.

In the center is the living room. One descends from an entrance balcony into a two-story space overlooking a terrace. Here, on the lower level, the main elements of the house are linked—living room, dining room, small art gallery, and library. Three separate staircases lead to the bedroom wings above.

On one level the house offers privacy and separation; on another the whole family comes together.

The five outdoor spaces—entrance court, pool court, service court, master-bedroom terrace, and living-room terrace with reflecting pool—are all clearly defined extensions of the interior spaces. The exterior is white stucco. Pocket windows allow full sheets of glass and screen to disappear into the walls.

1 Entrance court
2 Breezeway
3 Garage and service entrance
4 Daughters' bedroom/ sitting
5 Master bedroom suite
6 Entrance balcony
7 Open to below
8 Son's bedroom/sitting
9 Double-height living-and-dining room
10 Gallery
11 Library
12 Kitchen
13 Servants' quarters
14 Utility/service
15 Pool court
16 Service court
17 Master-bedroom terrace
18 Living-room terrace with reflecting pool
19 Future bridge and gazebo

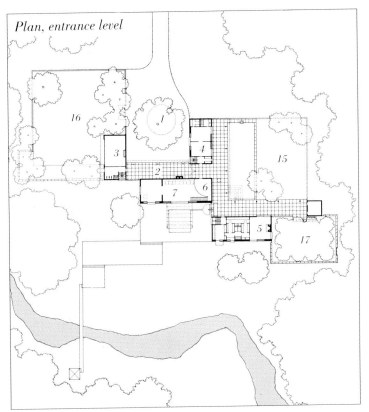

Plan, entrance level

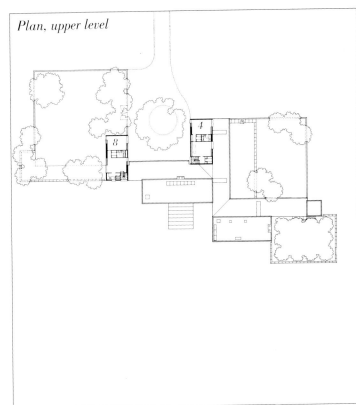

Plan, upper level

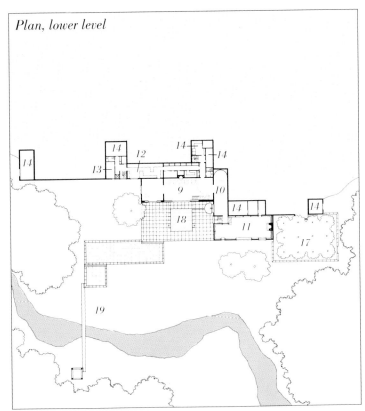

Plan, lower level

0   40   80 ft

Opposite: The terrace for the living room (at left, with pocket window) overlooks a reflecting pool. Beyond the pool is the art gallery with breezeway above and master-bedroom staircase to the right.

Below: Art gallery.

Bottom: Living room with entrance balcony.

Overleaf: The dining room is at the center, with the breezeway to the garage at left and the living-room terrace at right.

Garden Library

Upperville, Virginia, 1975–1983

In 1958 Mary and I went to Mykonos. We had been to Athens and had seen the clarity of classic Greek architecture, but I think Mykonos had a stronger effect on my style. Here was continuous stone architecture—roofs, walls, domes, barrel vaults, streets, outdoor steps—all painted white, all built over time on sloping hillsides. Years later, in 1975, I finally found a client who would paint stone. She sent me books on Portuguese farmhouses and asked me to do a private library on rolling farmland in Virginia.

There are two buildings, a high-ceilinged library with beautiful bound folios on full-height shelves surrounded by white stone and bold modern paintings and a two-story tower for a collection of rare china. Inside and out the stone is painted white.

1 *Path from house*
2 *Lower terrace*
3 *Hall*
4 *China collection*
5 *Meeting room*
6 *Stacks*
7 *Mechanical*
8 *Double-height library*
9 *Balcony*
10 *Study*
11 *Lawn*
12 *Upper terrace*
13 *Orchard*

First overleaf: View from the south, with library, lower terrace, and at left, china tower.

Second overleaf: View from the west, showing two-story library windows and china tower at right.

Third overleaf: View from the north, with library at left and china tower at right.

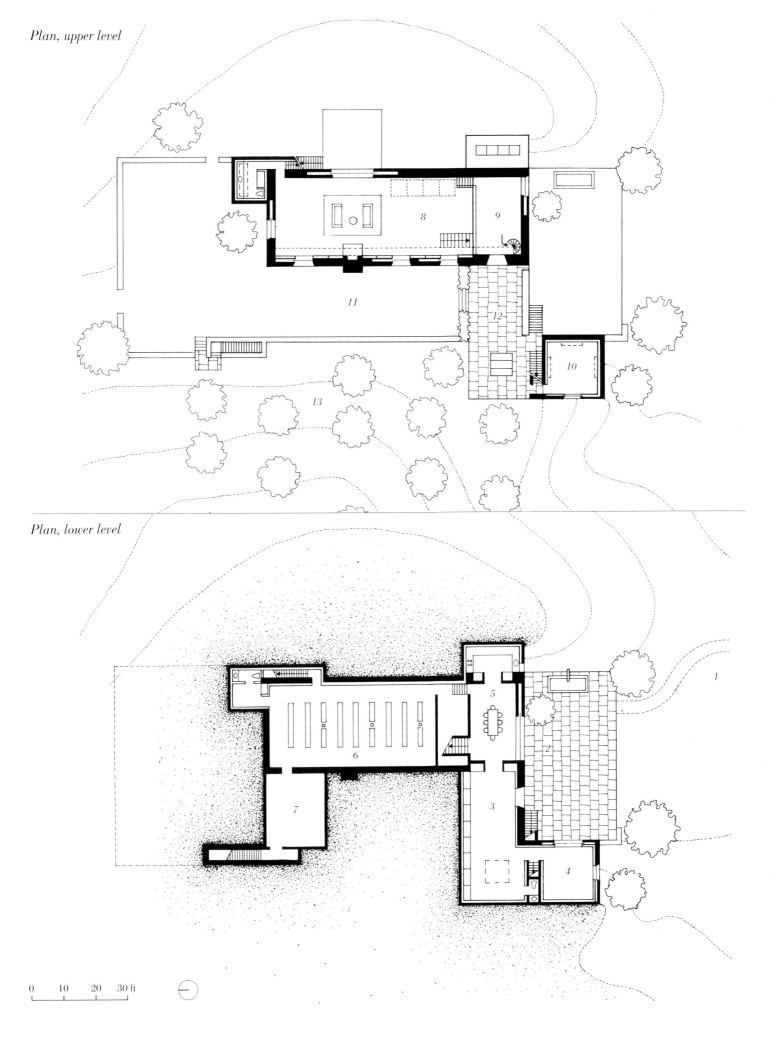

Plan, upper level

Plan, lower level

0   10   20   30 ft

Haystack Mountain School of Crafts

Deer Isle, Maine, 1958–1961
Visitors Center, 1979

*Below left: The genesis for
the forms of Haystack was
this first design for the
Osborn Studio, in 1950.*

One of the happiest jobs of my career was Haystack—
an arts and crafts summer school on Deer Isle, Maine. I
remember first walking onto the site and looking down
the rocky wooded slope to the sea. I wondered whether
we should build at the top or down near the shore. Then
it came to me: we could build *on* the slope, with a long
flight of steps perpendicular to the horizon. Studios and
sleeping units would branch out from each side.

The site is absolutely beautiful—tall spruce trees
against the sea, granite slopes, moss, and lichen. The
buildings, set on stilts, are interspersed with wood
decks. The idea was not to disturb the ground in any
way. There are two basic building types: sleeping units
with ribbon windows facing the sea and peaked
windows on the sides; and studios with tall windows for
north light and, again, ribbon windows facing the sea.
(These forms were adapted from an idea I had had for a
studio a few years before—a simple volumetric form
combining triangular and square geometry.)

It became apparent that we were designing a village
with a main "street" leading to the sea, dining hall and
offices at the top, studios and decks branching out on
side streets, and clusters of living units nestled in the
woods. The design provides separation for work and
living. The cost in 1960 with only rough studs inside
was about five dollars per square foot.

Haystack is now over thirty years old—years of hard
wear, reshingling, additions here and there, including a
foundry. One of the side streets was extended to add
more cottages. In 1979 we built a visitors center and
parking to direct the many summer visitors and their
cars away from the front door. With all of this, Haystack
remains a wonderfully poetic place to teach and learn.
In 1994 Haystack received the American Institute of
Architects Twenty-Five-Year Award.

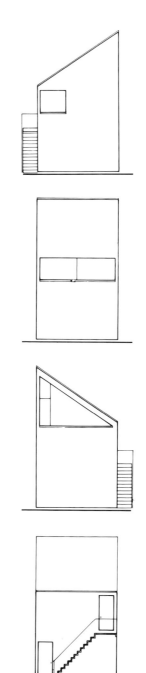

1 Office
2 Dining hall
3 Kitchen
4 Service shed
5 Luxury cabins
6 Carpentry shop
7 Pottery shop
8 Graphic shop
9 Weaving shop
10 Women's dormitory
11 Women's cabins
12 Bathrooms
13 Men's cabins
14 Men's dormitory
15 Faculty cabins
16 Outlook to sea
17 Visitors center: breezeway
18 Visitors center: gallery

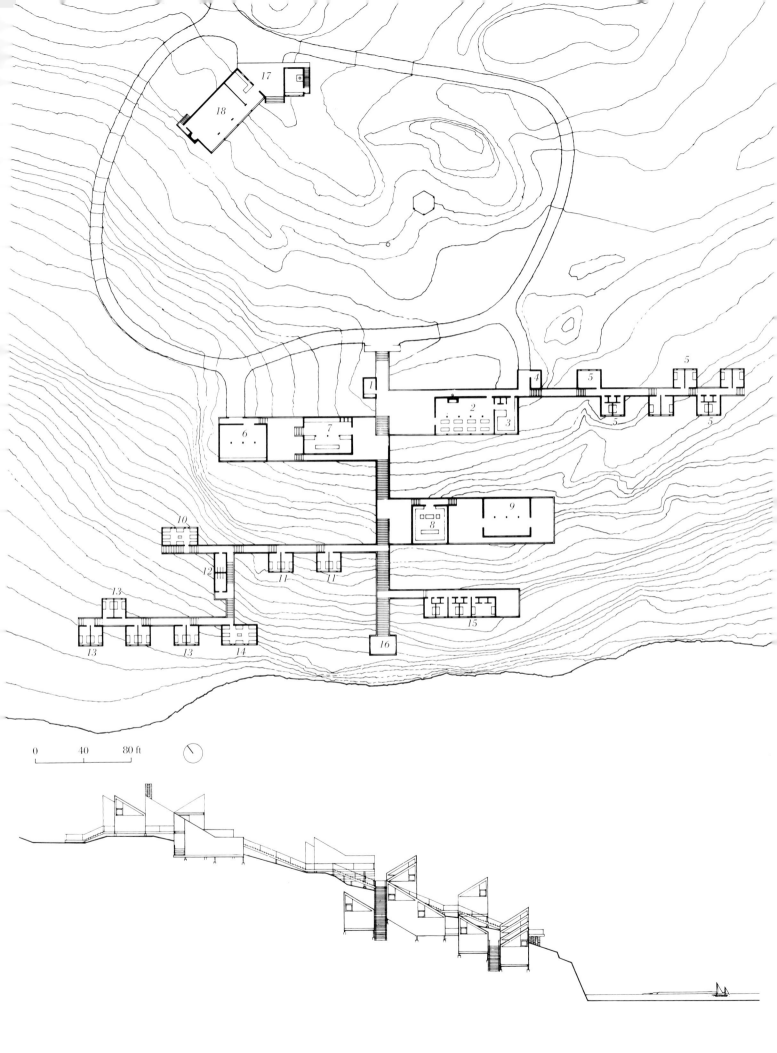

17
18

5
5
4
1
6
7
2
3
5
5
5
8
9
10
12
11
11
13
15
13
13
14
16

0   40   80 ft

Below: Sleeping unit with ribbon window facing the sea and peaked window looking up to the trees.

77

Camp Hidden Valley

Sharpe Reservation, Fishkill, New York, 1960–1961

From 1953 to 1961 I did several camps for the *New York Herald Tribune* Fresh Air Fund—post-and-lintel structures, tents on platforms, screened pavilions, and occasional rustic structures built of rocks and branching trees (see the Chronology).

Hidden Valley is a camp for handicapped children. The site plan is compact, with everything within easy walking distance: a central square surrounded by an administration building, a clinic, an outdoor stage, and a high-ceilinged dining pavilion. The columns and branching beams in the dining room recall a grove of trees.

A short distance away are the sleeping quarters, clustered in groups of three like tobacco barns.

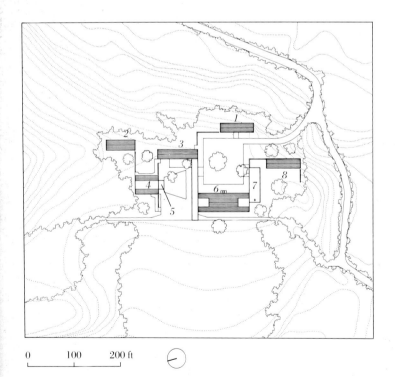

0   100   200 ft

Below and opposite: A typical cluster of sleeping units, with double-height rooms at the ends and skylit balcony space in the center.

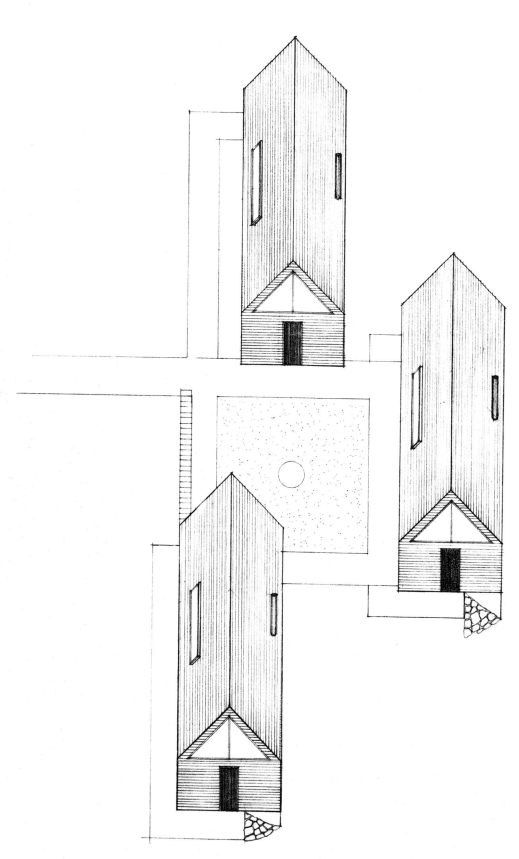

Dormitories, St. Paul's School

Concord, New Hampshire, 1959–1962

Overleaf: The boys' rooms step down the site, with single masters' apartments above and three-story married masters' houses at the ends.

Our problem here was to design a boys' dormitory in the center of an old campus. St. Paul's School has an elm-shaded street leading gently downhill through the campus. Along this street are the oldest buildings: the Victorian rectory, a Gothic chapel, a drum-shaped ice house—delicate, low-scale buildings. It seemed unthinkable to introduce a typical three-story block dormitory anywhere along this street. What we did was design a chain of *one-story* dormitories linking the old buildings and redefining the street.

The boys' rooms are all on the first floor. At certain points the buildings step down a half level—to follow the site—and on the half level *above* are apartments for unmarried masters. At the end of each dormitory are houses for married masters with families.

Tipped square windows light upper rooms under the sloping roofs. Deep red brick walls and copper roofs harmonize with the Victorian surroundings.

1 Entrance
2 Two-story master's house (garage below)
3 Single master's suite one-half level above
4 Boys' bedrooms
5 Rectory
6 School house
7 Ice house

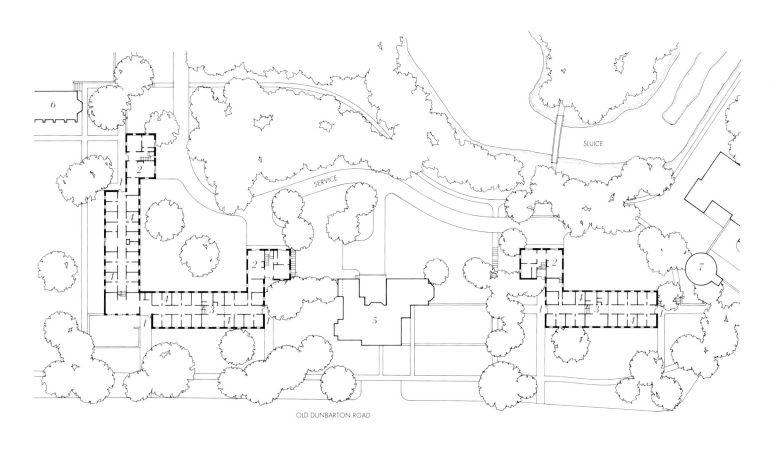

SLUICE

SERVICE

OLD DUNBARTON ROAD

Elevation from Old Dunbarton Road

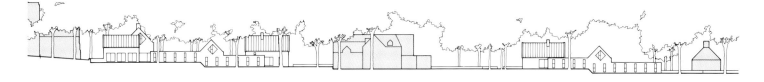

Elevation from sluice

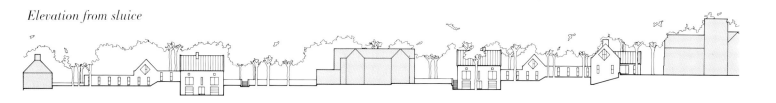

0   40   80 ft

Opposite: A dormitory entrance is at left, and a married master's house at center.

Below: Married masters' houses at left and right.

Bottom: The view along Old Dunbarton Road with the ice house at right.

Library, Music, and Art Building, Emma Willard School

Troy, New York, 1963–1967, 1971

Here we designed a tripartite building for the library and music and art departments, each separated by small courtyards. The idea was to promote interaction among these disciplines.

Again, the challenge was to harmonize with older buildings. We built of matching stone and kept the scale modest. Working *with* the old Gothic buildings, we composed a whole new campus space—a quadrangle.

On the other hand our building is abstract. The windows are paired squares, tipped squares, semicircular arches—all very simple geometry.

1 Entrance
2 Library
3 Music classroom
4 Art studio
5 Chapel
6 Classroom building
7 Future connecting link
 and entrance

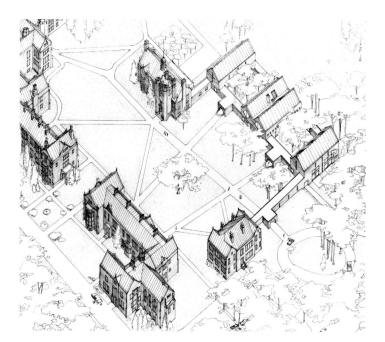

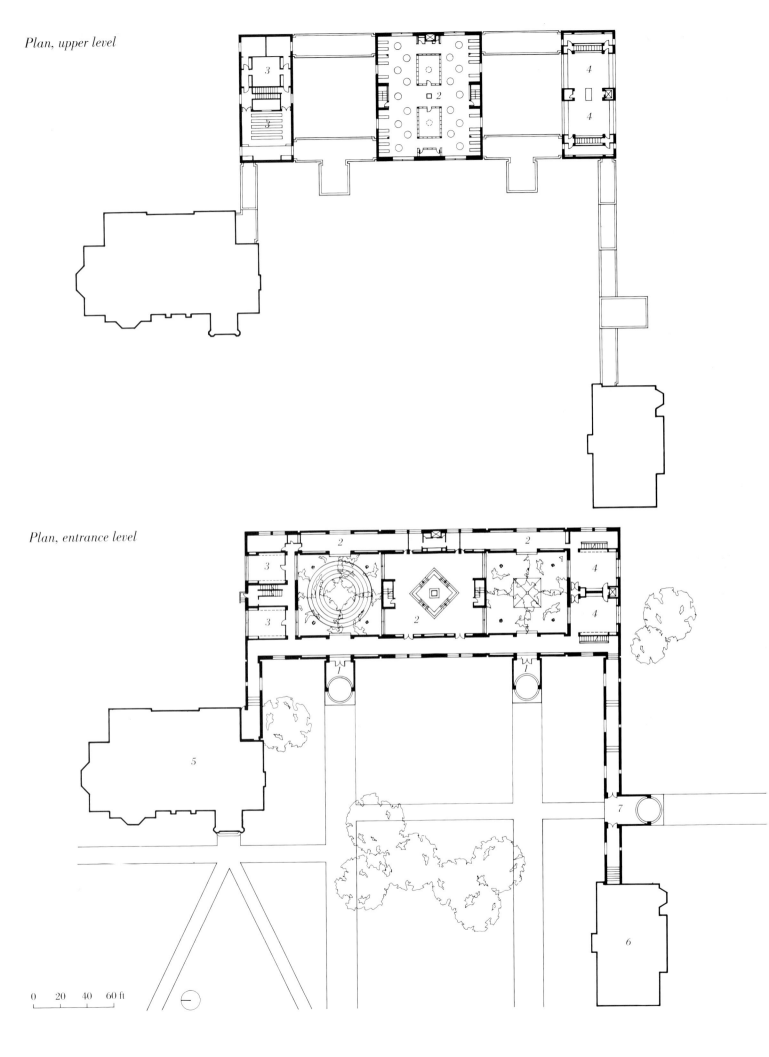

Plan, upper level

Plan, entrance level

0   20   40   60 ft

Faculty Apartments, Emma Willard School

Troy, New York 1963–1966

In housing design it is important to break down the scale—to create an organic cluster where one senses the parts as well as the whole. This is "village" architecture. Many times, whether in school dormitories, or apartments, or even single-family houses, I have tried to humanize the design by breaking down the scale.

The Emma Willard faculty housing, built of broken-faced concrete block, suggests a pueblo village. The three-story apartments step downhill with outdoor terraces on all levels. One enters the middle floor and moves up to penthouses or down to garden apartments. The mass, as in pueblo architecture, is softened by the stepped profile. Each apartment has its own identity, its own sense of place. Yet the whole cluster is a coherent form wedded to the hillside.

First overleaf: View from the west.

Second overleaf: Entrance from the west.

Third overleaf: View from the east showing stepped terraces.

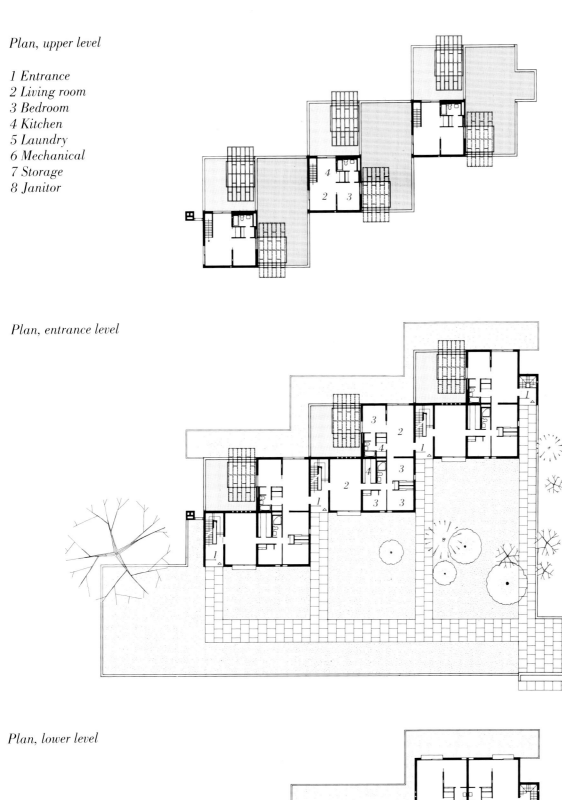

Plan, upper level

1 Entrance
2 Living room
3 Bedroom
4 Kitchen
5 Laundry
6 Mechanical
7 Storage
8 Janitor

Plan, entrance level

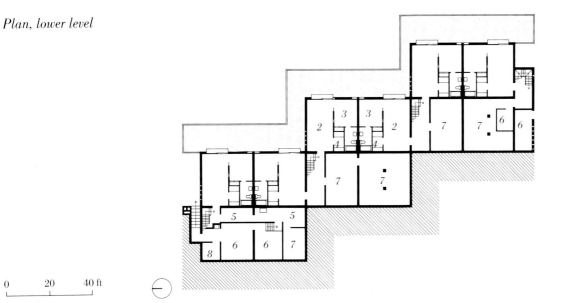

Plan, lower level

0   20   40 ft

Visual Arts Center, Bowdoin College

Brunswick, Maine, 1972–1976

1 Visual Arts Center
2 Walker Art Museum
3 Chapel
4 Underground gallery

Opposite: Studios overlook the entrance. The Upjohn chapel is seen through the "archway."

Bowdoin College has a traditional American campus—detached buildings placed formally around a green. We were asked to design a large building for the visual arts department, functionally connected to one of the old buildings—the Walker Art Museum by McKim, Mead and White. Quite apart from what this would do to the classic symmetry of the museum, we thought it would harm the rhythm of the buildings around the green.

Next to the museum was an open space, a missing tooth so to speak. However, this open space was precious; it centered on the chapel designed by Richard Upjohn. Bowdoin students had filed through this open space to the chapel from time immemorial.

After much debate, it was decided that we should build in the open space, to *bridge* the walk to the chapel, and construct an underground connection to the museum. The Visual Arts Center became an open archway to the campus with high-ceilinged studio space above. The connection to the museum below grade is ideal for temporary exhibits.

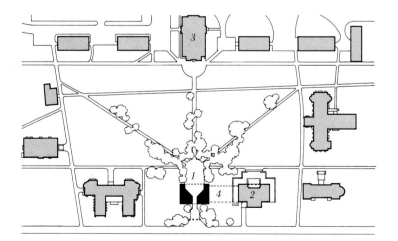

0   100   200   300 ft

Plan, third floor

1 Covered entrance
2 Gallery
3 Picture study room
4 Classroom
5 Lounge
6 Secretarial/reception
7 Offices
8 Seminar room
9 Library
10 Studio
11 High-ceilinged studio
12 Private studios

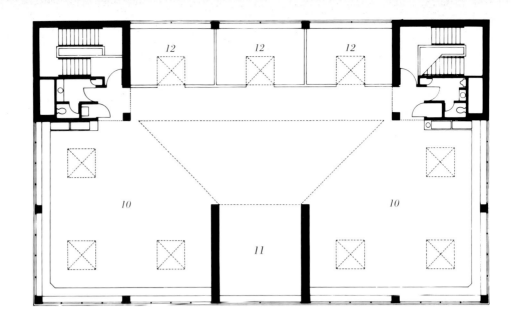

Plan, second floor

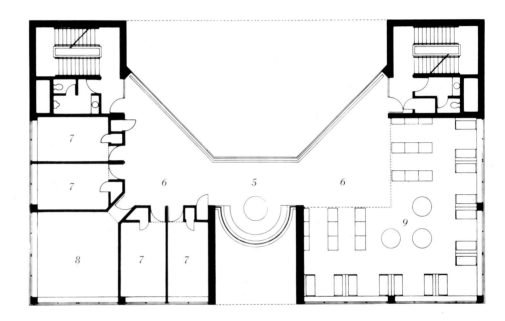

Plan, first floor

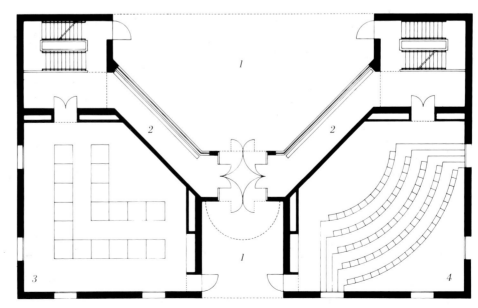

0   10   20 ft

Computer Center, Bryn Mawr College

Bryn Mawr, Pennsylvania, 1984–1986

1 Work spaces and terminals
2 Library
3 Offices
4 Computer equipment
5 Storage
6 Mechanical
7 Lower-level service
8 Classroom

Bryn Mawr College has an elegant Victorian Gothic campus. To minimize the bulk of a large computer facility, we placed the laboratories underground, around a small landscaped court. Service is from the street at a lower level.

Above ground is a two-story classroom building. The siting (aligned with adjacent buildings), massing (a cubic building with steep roof and low eaves), and material (granite and slate) are all contextual.

The exaggerated limestone squares at the corners recall the corner quoins of older campus buildings—without being direct quotations.

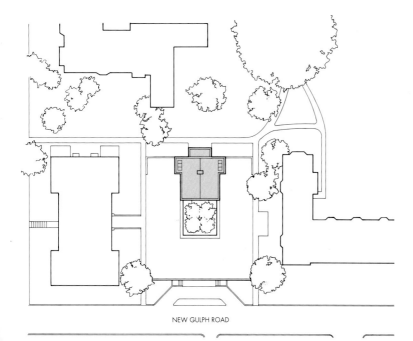

NEW GULPH ROAD

0   40   80 ft

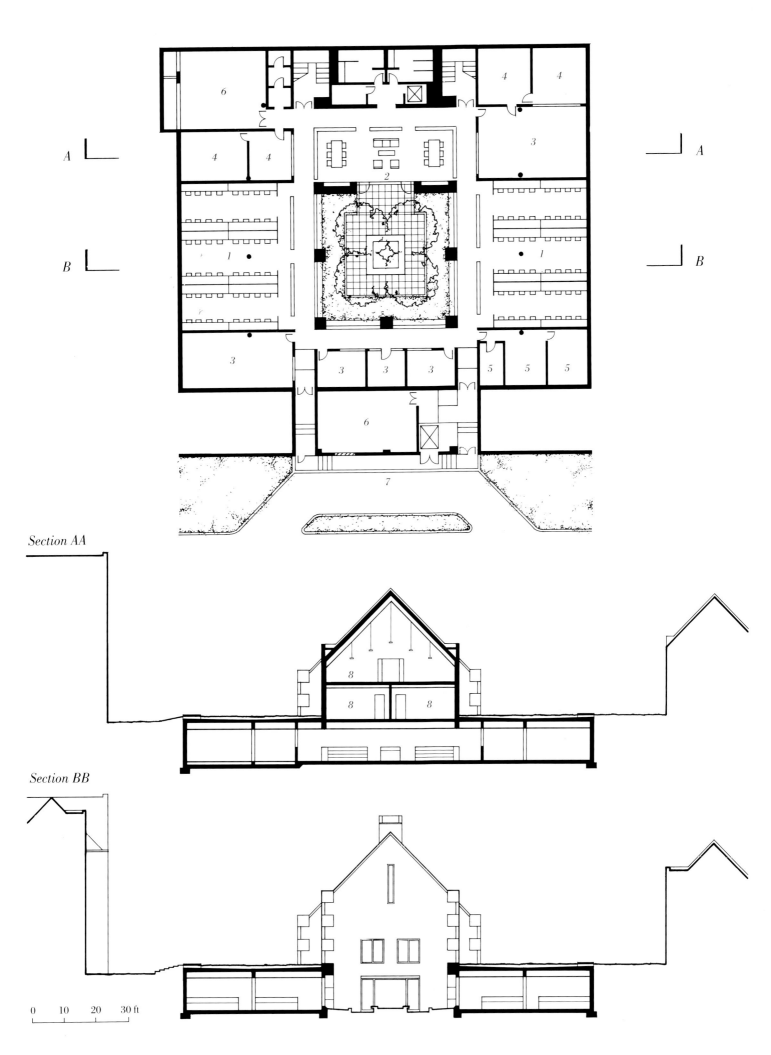

A   A

B   B

Section AA

Section BB

0   10   20   30 ft

Opposite: The computer center in context.

Below: The small landscaped court surrounded by below-grade computer laboratories.

Allen Library, University of Washington

Seattle, Washington, 1985–1991

Overleaf: View from HUB Yard.

At an interview for this project, a member of the selection committee pressed me for my thoughts. I suggested redefining the amorphous space in front of the student union and linking it *through* the new library to the main campus mall to the west. This called for a strong mass facing the union, possibly with a tower, and a major passageway through the building. In essence, this scheme was ultimately built. The green lawn between the union and the library has become a significant campus open space, and the arcade through the library a major campus thoroughfare.

Of course, one does not lightly put a hole through a library. Fortunately the librarian agreed to divide the collections and accepted two control points. Two basement floors contain compact stacks. Three floors bridge the arcade. The top floor has high-ceilinged conference rooms on the bridge and in the tower.

The campus architecture is largely collegiate Gothic. We exploited many features of adjacent buildings for details—patterned brick, terra-cotta spandrels, finials along upper parapets, and occasional steep-roofed towers. The result is harmonious: new and old fuse seamlessly.

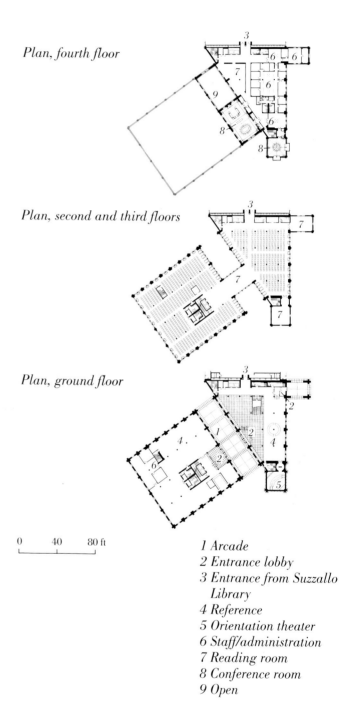

Plan, fourth floor

Plan, second and third floors

Plan, ground floor

0   40   80 ft

1 Arcade
2 Entrance lobby
3 Entrance from Suzzallo Library
4 Reference
5 Orientation theater
6 Staff/administration
7 Reading room
8 Conference room
9 Open

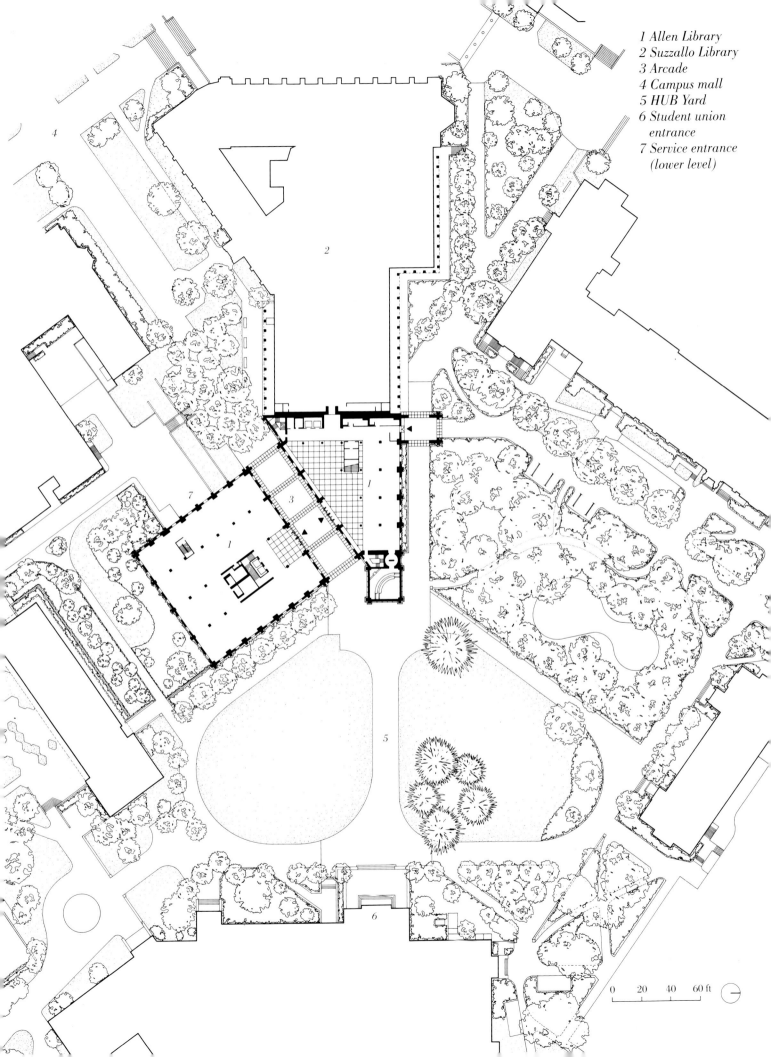

1 Allen Library
2 Suzzallo Library
3 Arcade
4 Campus mall
5 HUB Yard
6 Student union
  entrance
7 Service entrance
  (lower level)

0   20   40   60 ft

State University of
New York at Potsdam

1962–1973

In 1962 the Potsdam campus was a loose assortment of
separate buildings scattered around an enormous field.
Our solution links buildings to tighten the campus and
clearly define outdoor space. The classical binuclear
campus plan centers academic buildings around the
library and dormitories around the student union.

New classroom buildings with long low rooflines and
glazed hallways frame a great court. Diagonal walks
and groves of maples lead to the library that, with its
high reading room, marks the academic center.
Monumental gateways at each corner rise to the same
height as the library roof and provide formal entrances.

The student union, like the library, dominates in
both axial placement and massing. It unites four
existing buildings and provides the centerpiece for all
dormitories, old and new. New dormitories branch
out to the south, each with its own courtyard and high-
rise tower.

Later, Giovanni Pasanella, Joseph Merz, and Richard
Moger (all of whom had worked in my office) were
individually commissioned to design buildings within
the master plan. In 1973 we designed the Crane Music
Center, consisting of studios, classrooms, theater, and
concert hall on the eastern axis.

1 Library
2 Student union
3 Fine arts building
4 Classroom building
5 Administration building
   (Giovanni Pasanella)
6 Lecture halls

7 Science building
   (Giovanni Pasanella and
   Joseph Merz)
8 Dormitory
9 Dormitory (Joseph Merz)
10 Crane Music Center
11 Service
12 Student union expansion
13 Dormitory

■ Original buildings

▨ Master plan buildings

☐ Future buildings

Opposite: This aerial photo shows the dormitory clusters around the student union and the academic buildings around the library. The Crane Music Center, under construction, is at left.

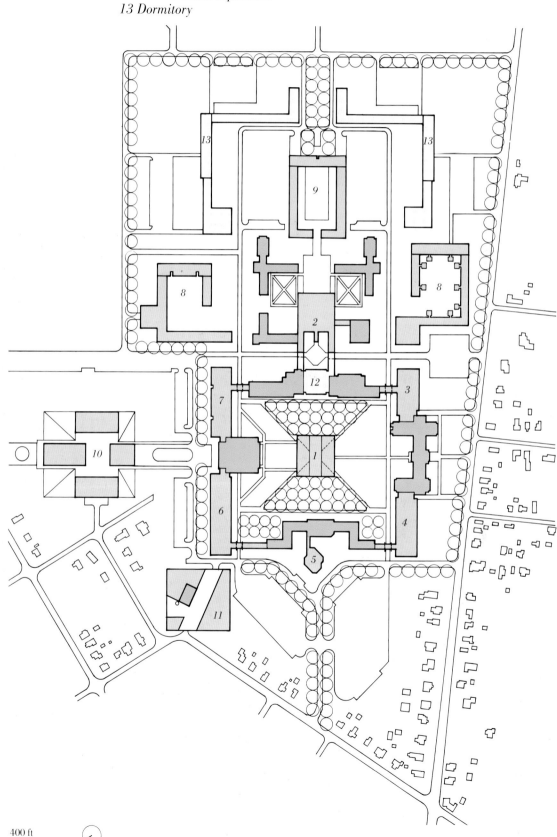

0   200   400 ft

State University of New York at Purchase

1966–1977

Purchase is a liberal-arts college with strong emphasis on the performing arts. The campus is dominated by a nine-hundred-foot-long court. At the western end, the Performing Arts Center, a cluster of four theaters with stage towers, rises above the rest of the campus. At the center is the library, with a Henry Moore sculpture in front. At the eastern end is an open meadow flanked by dormitories. At the far end of the meadow is a gymnasium built into the side of a hill. Thus, from east to west across the campus a formal chain of buildings and open spaces serves the entire college community.

Covered walks with broad avenues of shade trees run along each side of the great court. Perpendicular to these walks are pedestrian streets spaced at regular intervals. The various academic buildings occupy the blocks between these streets. Each department (humanities, social sciences, sciences, visual arts and gallery, theater arts, music, and dance) has an entrance from the central court and from the pedestrian streets. Each can expand to the north or south.

This is a compact *pedestrian* campus. Parking fans out below the Performing Arts Center. Basement corridors serve all academic buildings. The plaza bridges Lincoln Avenue. Acres of open meadow land have been preserved all around.

The overall form is clear. The great court, pedestrian streets, and uniform brown brick all make for unity. However, there is also great diversity. The architects commissioned—seven firms in all—did as they wished with their blocks. Several were former employees of my office—Giovanni Pasanella, Robert Siegel, and Charles Gwathmey. Relationships among projects are free, often accidental. The result is a little town set in five hundred acres of green fields.

1 Great court
2 Performing Arts Center
3 Library, post office, bookstore
4 Meadow
5 Gymnasium
6 Cooling tower
7 Student activities A
8 Humanities building (Venturi and Rauch)
9 Roy R. Neuberger Museum of Art (Philip Johnson and John Burgee)
10 Visual arts instructional facility (The Architects Collaborative)
11 Theater arts instructional facility (not built)
12 Music instructional facility
13 Dance instructional facility (Gunnar Birkerts & Associates)
14 Natural science building (Paul Rudolph)
15 Social science building (Venturi and Rauch)
16 Student activities B
17 Dormitory (original scheme, not built; Giovanni Pasanella)
18 Dormitory (Gwathmey, Henderson, and Siegel)
19 Service (Gwathmey, Henderson, and Siegel)
20 Parking

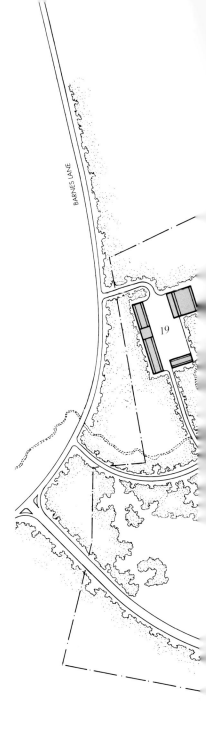

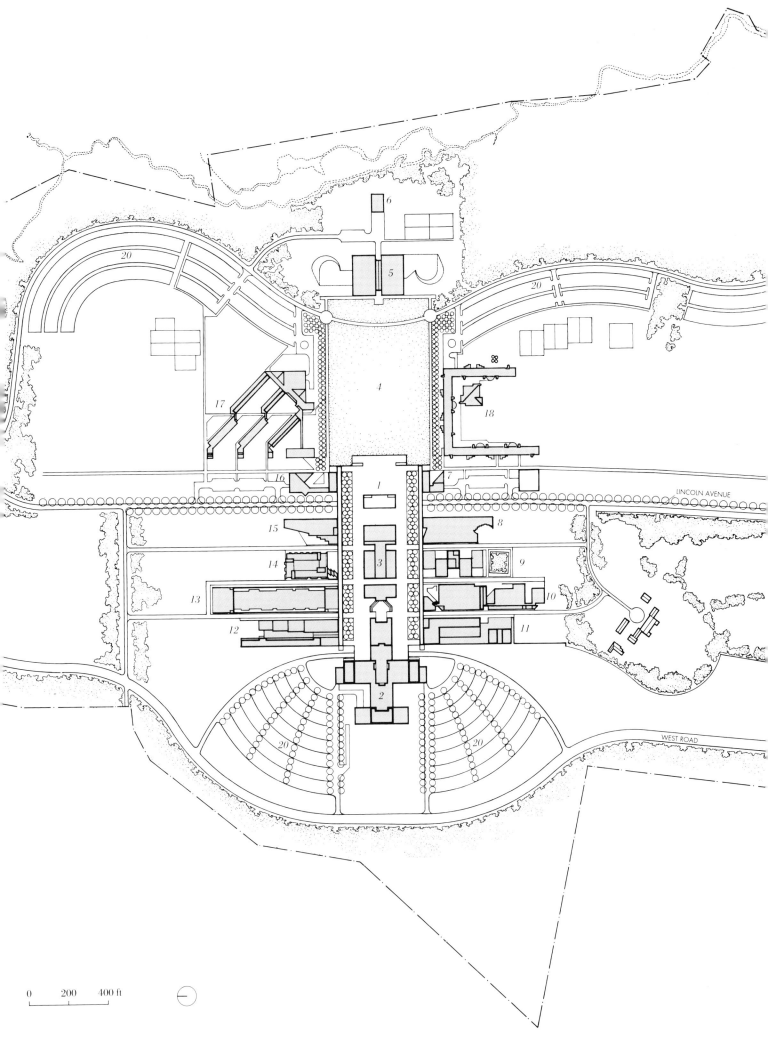

LINCOLN AVENUE

WEST ROAD

0   200   400 ft

Below: Music building and stage towers from the west.

Opposite: Stage towers in the Performing Arts Center.

Bottom: Maples and covered walk flanking great court.

Opposite: Library roof planes.

Below: Gymnasium entrance.

Bottom: Library with Henry Moore sculpture, seen from meadow.

Overleaf: Music building.

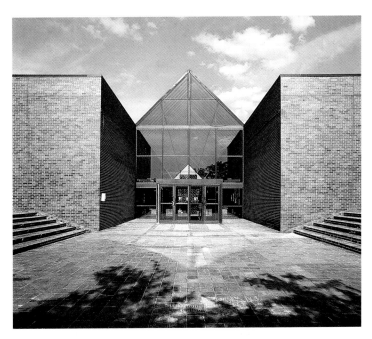

Indiana University/ Purdue University at Indianapolis

1976–1994

Below: The students call the pedestrian bridges "gerbil tubes."

Opposite: Natatorium.

In 1976 the IUPUI campus stretched over several blocks of downtown Indianapolis. Two major high-speed avenues cut through from east to west. IUPUI is a commuter campus, with parking lots everywhere. Major expansion was anticipated, and a master plan was needed.

Our plan creates a pedestrian zone between the two avenues. Ample garages *outside* this zone are linked by pedestrian bridges over the avenues to the second level of the academic buildings. Buildings connect so that one walks indoors across the campus from the hotel/conference center, through classroom buildings, past the library, and on to the gymnasium.

Linking the buildings changes the spatial character of the campus. Instead of separate building blocks, it becomes a series of framed courtyards. New classroom buildings are raised on pilotis so that the pedestrian space runs through from court to court, allowing one to feel the ground plane sweeping across the campus.

Focal buildings are the natatorium (a great indoor swimming stadium), the hotel/conference center, and the recently completed library.

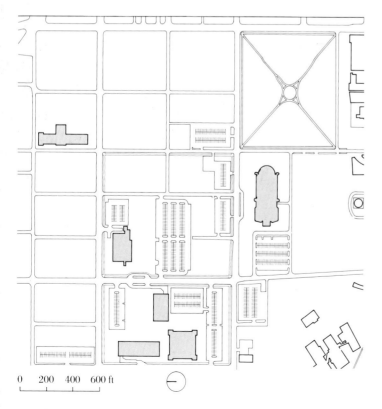

0   200   400   600 ft

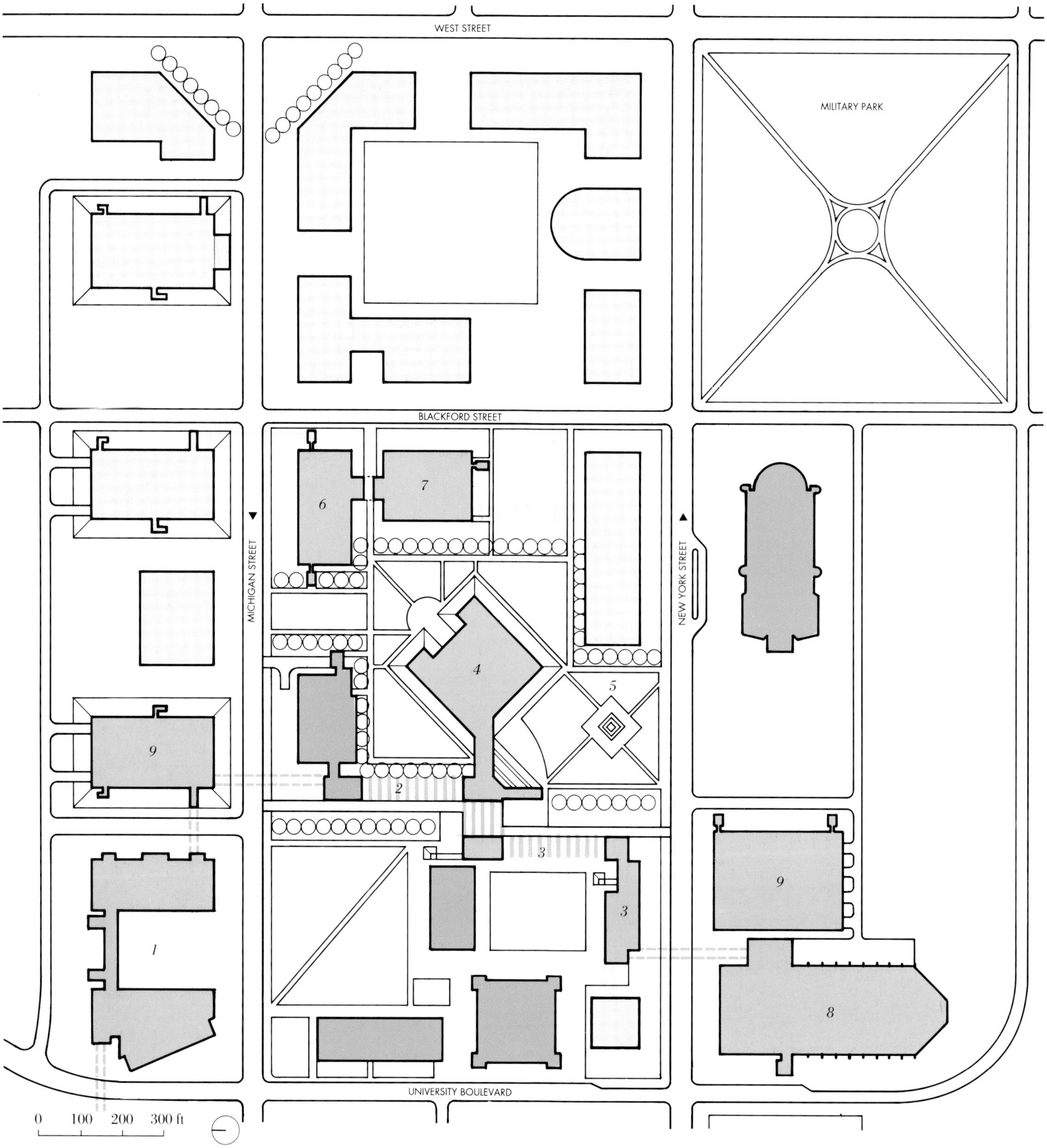
WEST STREET
MILITARY PARK
BLACKFORD STREET
MICHIGAN STREET
NEW YORK STREET
UNIVERSITY BOULEVARD
1
2
3
3
4
5
6
7
8
9
9
9
0 100 200 300 ft

1 Hotel and conference center
2 Business school/planning and environmental administration
3 Education school/social work
4 Library
5 Fountain
6 Science, engineering, and technology building, phase II
7 Science, engineering, and technology building, phase III
8 Natatorium
9 Garage

Original buildings

Master plan buildings

Future buildings

Building on stilts

Pedestrian bridge

Top: The library under
construction, with the
connection to the pedestrian
bridge level at left. (The main
library entrance is at grade
on the northeast.)

Above: Library atrium.

Christian Theological Seminary

Indianapolis, Indiana, 1961–1987

Master planning for Christian Theological Seminary began in 1961. The campus was built in phases as funds allowed and was completed in 1987 with the dedication of Sweeney Chapel (see page 190).

From the start we decided to build not separate buildings but a continuous chain. The S-shaped plan defines two outdoor spaces: an entrance court facing the street and a quiet open square overlooking the flood plane of the White River eighty feet below. At one end are the social functions: the lounge, dining hall, and theater. Next comes a procession of rooms around the great square—offices, seminar rooms, lecture halls, and library. Finally, hanging over the bluff is the chapel—a block with a bell tower anchoring the corner of the campus.

The materials, appropriately, continue throughout: cream-colored pebble-concrete exteriors and white plaster interiors set off with bold commissioned art by George Ortman, Victor Vasarely, Ben Nicholson, Arnaldo Pomodoro, and others. The entire campus appears as a unit, with the bell tower and chapel rising above.

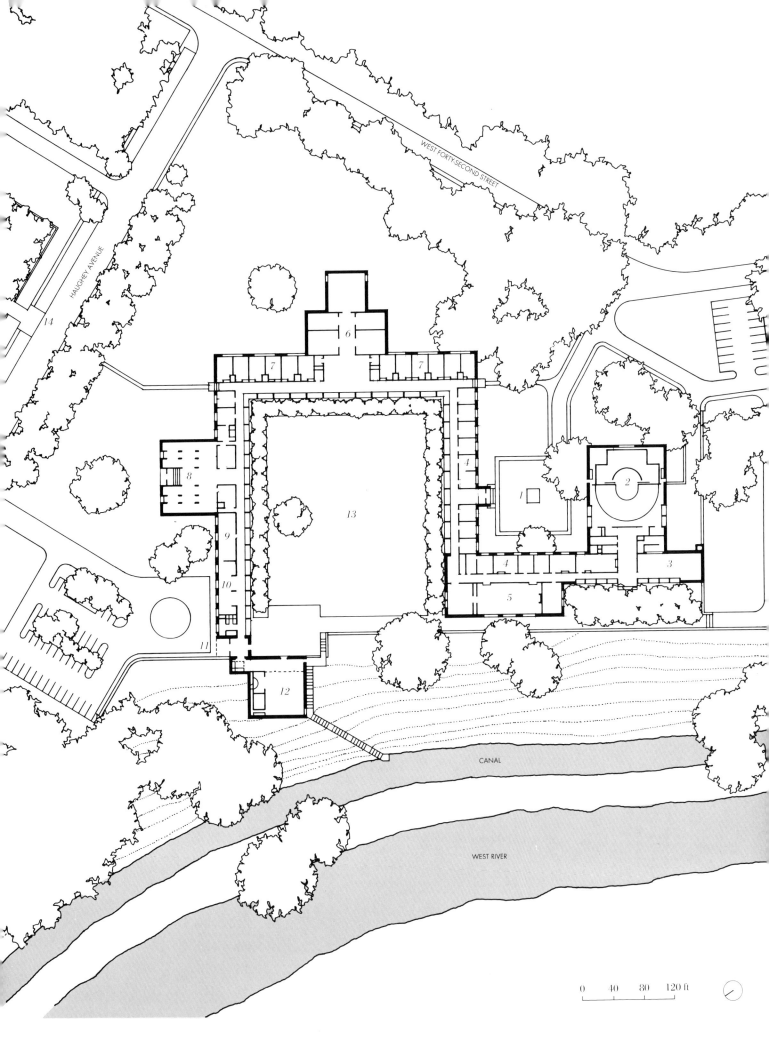

WEST FORTY-SECOND STREET

HAUGHEY AVENUE

14

6

7   7

8

4

1   2

9

3

10   4

5

13

11

12

CANAL

WEST RIVER

0   40   80   120 ft

Opposite: Precast columns, gravel borders, and shade trees frame the great court.

Below: Dining hall.

Bottom: Lecture and seminar rooms, with faculty offices above.

Below: Student lounge.   *Bottom: Greek theater with thrust stage.*

New England Merchants National Bank

Boston, Massachusetts, 1963–1970

The New England Merchants National Bank was one of the first Boston skyscrapers—a sleek tower with sculpted top and base. The building stands on sloping ground. An arcade runs along the higher side, facing a narrow pedestrian street. This arcade centers on two important civic buildings—the Old State House to the south and the new city hall to the north. One enters the tower from this arcade, directly onto the balcony of the two-story main banking hall. A Larry Rivers mural, *Boston Massacre,* hangs at one end.

At the top of the tower a restaurant with a stepped-down floor and deeply recessed windows looks out to the sea. Above this is the executive office floor, with boardrooms, conference rooms, etc., opening to a landscaped roof terrace.

All floors, including the top and base, convey the building's volumetric proportions.

1 Banking hall
2 Arcade
3 Ames Building
4 Old State House
5 New city hall
6 Future pedestrian bridge

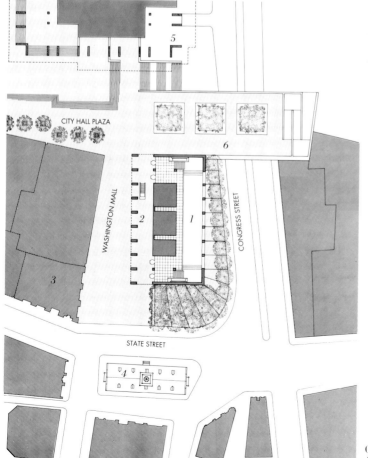

0   80   160   240 ft

1 Banking hall
2 Tellers
3 Lobby
4 Loading dock
5 Bank offices
6 Vault
7 Arcade
8 Subway
9 Open to banking
   hall below
10 Bar
11 Lounge
12 Restaurant
13 Kitchen
14 Offices
15 Terrace

Plan, arcade and
upper banking hall

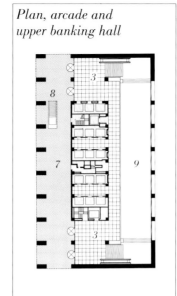

Plan, rooftop restaurant

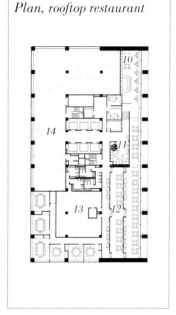

Plan, executive office floor

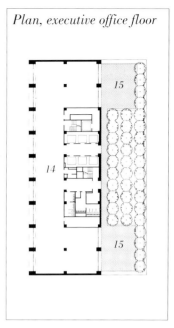

Plan, main banking floor

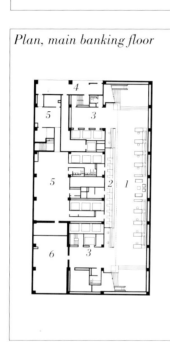

Plan, typical office floor

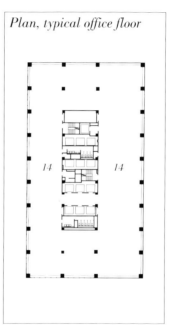

0   80   160 ft

East elevation

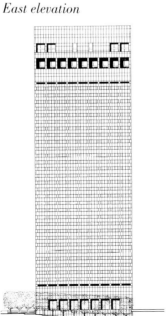

South elevation

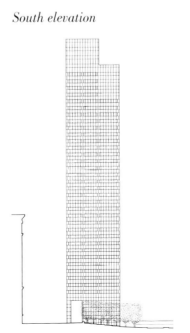

West elevation

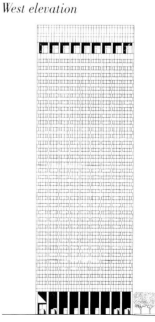

0   100   200   300 ft

Below: Looking south, the arcade centers on the Old State House.

Opposite: View from Congress Street past the new city hall.

Crown Center

Kansas City, Missouri, 1967–1972

1 *Existing Hallmark buildings*
2 *Office complex*
3 *Fountain plaza*
4 *Shopping center*
5 *Hotel (Harry Weese and Associates)*
6 *Residential, Phase I (Norman Fletcher, The Architects Collaborative)*

In the 1950s Hallmark, the Kansas City greeting-card company, acquired eighty-five acres around the company headquarters as part of a massive urban renewal program. We were asked to do a master plan and then, with architects Harry Weese and Norman Fletcher, to design the buildings.

The scope of the plan is ambitious: office buildings, shops, theaters, restaurants, hotels, apartments, and more. Our master plan called for a great open space terracing downhill in front of the existing Hallmark buildings with below-grade parking for 2,300 cars. A hotel, a shopping center bridging the street, and a chain of office buildings overlook the central square, a fountain plaza with a grid of water plumes capable of various displays. The fountain can be turned off and the flat cobblestone pavement used for special events like concerts and fairs.

The office complex (626,000 square feet, seven stories) is a chain divided into five separate buildings, each on a different level, with breezeway entrances leading through to the central square; the design gives the tenants freedom to expand horizontally as well as vertically in the complex. The chain steps downhill along the curve of the street. Cream-colored precast cladding gives the complex continuity.

A slender office tower, unfortunately never built, was to terminate the chain of offices and frame the entrance to the square.

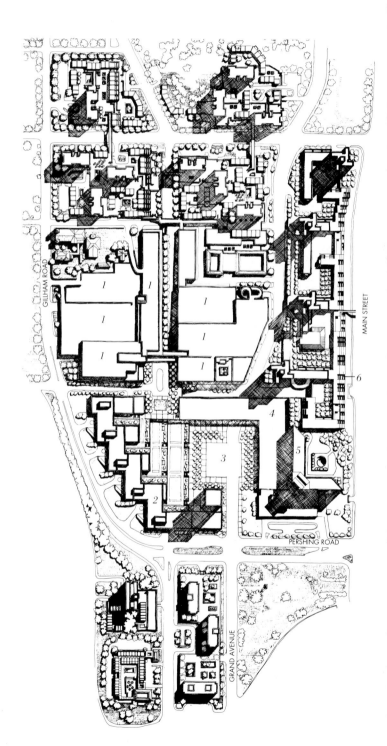

0   200   400 ft

Americas/Far East Headquarters, IBM World Trade Corporation

Mount Pleasant, New York, 1972–1975

The rural site for this office building is adjacent to a beautiful conservation park, so we were determined not to build a glaring suburban misfit.

What we did build is a quiet, serpentine building, two stories high on the entrance side and stepping down to three on the rear. Dark green spandrels and floor-to-ceiling dark green glass overlook a long reflecting pool that follows the building's contours. The angles, dark facades, and reflections create illusions, yet the architecture is strong, gently capturing outdoor space.

Most of the building is devoted to an open office "landscape"—workstations subdivided with low partitions. Circulation is along the glass wall. Conference rooms, a library, and a few private offices extend along the entry wall. At the center is the main lobby with a cafeteria below. Service comes in underground, below the parking lot.

The open office plan here is more democratic than the usual rabbit warren of little private offices. As a workplace the building is unique: quiet, open, meandering space looks over meadows and water.

At focal points Ivan Chermayeff designed interesting "collections": collages of stamps, grains, fabrics, and spices extending the full wall height.

1 Entrance
2 Open office
3 Reflecting pool
4 Ramp down to service
5 Parking

First overleaf: The three-story facade is mirrored in the reflecting pool.

Second overleaf: The glazed corridor and open office landscape overlook the reflecting pool.

Third overleaf: The building and natural beauty of the site interlock.

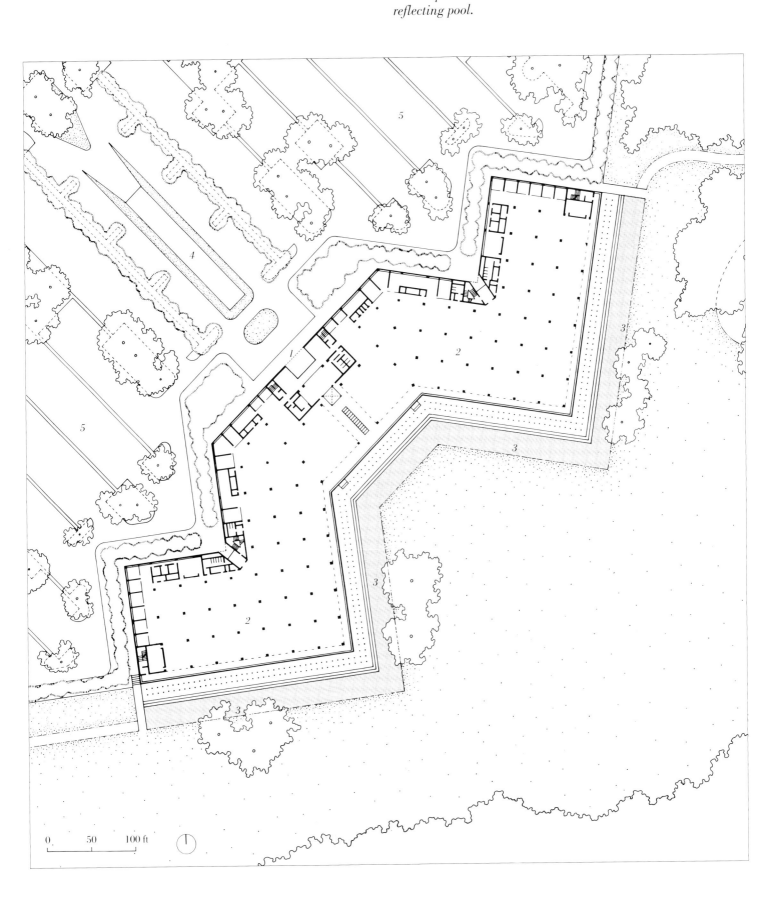

0   50   100 ft

IBM 590 Madison Avenue

New York, New York, 1973–1983

Overleaf: The corner at Fifty-seventh Street and Madison Avenue is cantilevered.

In 1973 New York City permitted developers to exceed legal limitations on allowable square feet if they provided certain benefits—such as public park space, through-block arcades, and setbacks facing south. This building is the successful result of collaboration between corporation, city, and architect: a facility that works well for IBM and provides a major amenity for the general public.

The tower itself is straightforward—a forty-three-story, green granite prismatic shaft. The tower is not set back from the street behind an empty plaza, as was the fashion at the time. Instead, it holds to the street line on the north and east to save as much open space as possible on the opposite, sunny side of the building. To provide a spacious entrance for IBM, the building cantilevers over the sidewalk. The omission of a corner column produces an unexpected sense of openness at what would otherwise be a crowded corner, Fifty-seventh Street and Madison Avenue.

The open space at the corner of Fifty-sixth Street features a low fountain designed by Michael Heizer.

The plan leaves the southwest half of the block entirely open. Here we built a greenhouse park shaded by giant clumps of bamboo. Along one side is a through-block arcade, thirty-five feet high. Sliding glass doors make it possible to open the arcade at each end except in the coldest weather, when the doors are closed and the greenhouse heated. The greenhouse provides access to the IBM tower, the IBM Gallery of Science and Art (stairs lead down to large subgrade galleries), the New York Botanical Garden shop, and next door, the Galeries Lafayette department store. IBM finances luncheon concerts. There is a snack bar, as well as seats and benches for relaxation. The IBM block has become one of Manhattan's most important public parks.

1 Lobby
2 Gallery
3 New York Botanical Garden Shop
4 Greenhouse park
5 Kiosk
6 Through-block arcade
7 Galeries Lafayette
8 Fountain sculpture
9 Dining room
10 Servery
11 Kitchen
12 Bamboo canopy
13 Reception
14 Conference room
15 Offices

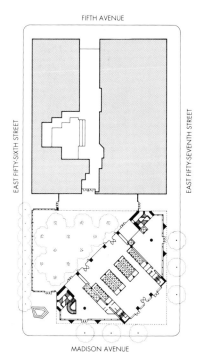

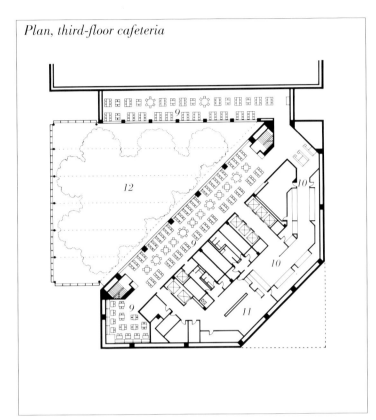

Plan, third-floor cafeteria

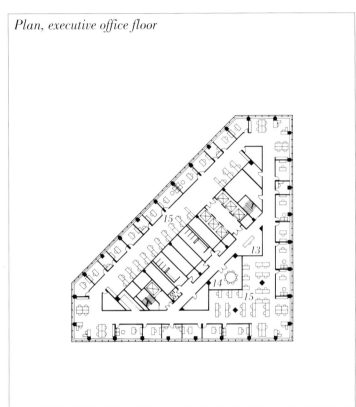

Plan, executive office floor

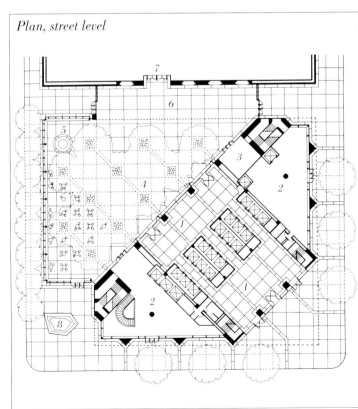

Plan, street level

0   25   50   75 ft

599 Lexington Avenue

New York, New York, 1981–1986

This building stands in a congested part of the city,
surrounded by buildings of all heights. How could our
design be contextual and also assert a presence of its
own?

The site is roughly square. At street level we sliced
off the northwest corner of our building to create an
entrance plaza amplifying the open space around the
Citicorp building to the north. At six stories, we sliced
off the southwest corner to respect low facades across
Fifty-second Street. These two cuts produced a bold
prow with views up and down Lexington Avenue. At
thirty-three stories, the approximate level of buildings
across Lexington, we cut back the prow to produce a
west facade in line with the Citicorp tower. Finally, at
forty-two stories, we sliced off the northeast and
southeast corners to produce a bold triangular top. We
called this "subtractive" massing. Office floors range
from seven thousand to thirty-one thousand square feet.

The distinctive skin consists of a silver-green aluminum
frame with circular columns at the corners to permit the
facades to "pivot" as the massing changes. The window
glass and spandrel glass are blue-green. The spandrel
glass is set six inches in front of white panels to give the
impression of depth. One reads the strong aluminum
frame; everything else is illusory.

A fifty-foot-high glass lobby with a Frank Stella
painting overlooks the entrance plaza. Glass-covered
stairs in the plaza lead down to a new subway concourse
with bold graphics by Ivan Chermayeff.

Plan, 42nd–47th floors

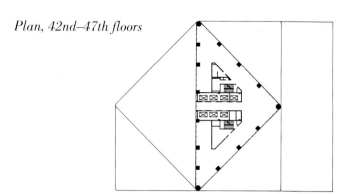

Plan, 33rd–41st floors

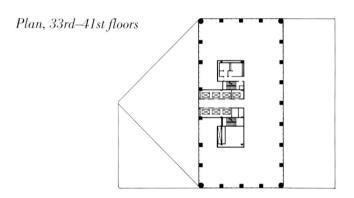

Plan, 6th–32nd floors

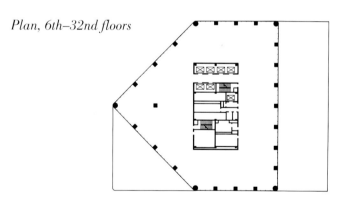

Plan, ground–5th floors

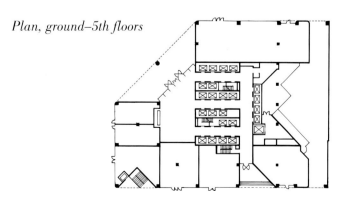

0   40   80 ft

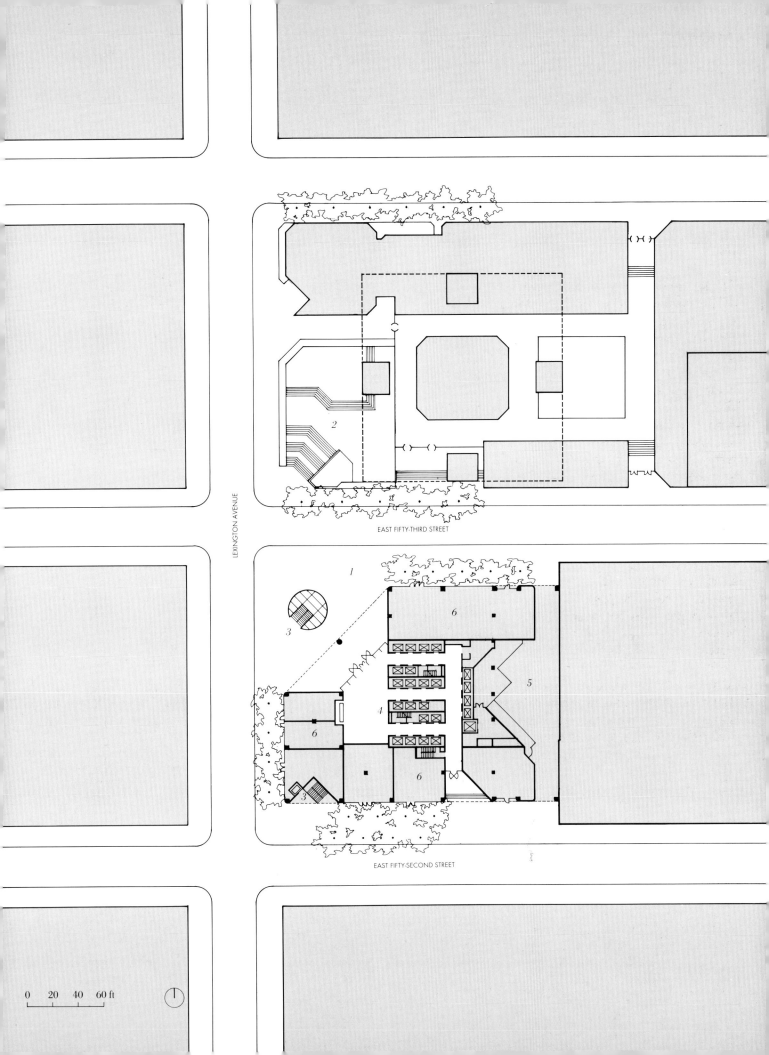

EAST FIFTY-THIRD STREET

LEXINGTON AVENUE

EAST FIFTY-SECOND STREET

0   20   40   60 ft

Thurgood Marshall
Federal Judiciary Building

Washington, D.C., 1988–1992

Above: The "keyhole" arrangement of windows, seen through the Union Station arcade.

Overleaf: Union Station and the Thurgood Marshall Federal Judiciary Building, from Columbus Circle.

1 *Entrance*
2 *Bamboo atrium*
3 *Lobby*
4 *Offices*
5 *Garage ramps*
6 *Open to atrium*
7 *Balcony terrace*
8 *Glass roof over atrium*

9 *Union Station*
10 *United States Post Office (now United States Postal Museum)*
11 *Thurgood Marshall Federal Judiciary Building*

Daniel Burnham's great Union Station with the civic space before it is a Washington landmark. To the west is the old Post Office, also by Burnham. The site to the east had long been empty. In the late 1980s it was dedicated for a new million-square-foot judiciary office building. The Architect of the Capitol conducted an invited design-build competition. We entered with Boston Properties as developer and won.

Our building picks up the main rhythms of the Burnham facades but not the decorative details. One might call this "abstract classicism." Granite blocks (three to sixteen inches thick) cast deep shadows. This is no paper-thin curtain wall.

The first three floors are grouped in a "keyhole" arrangement of windows separated by regular stone pilasters. Just below the cornice in what would be the frieze are horizontal windows, and the attic story features regularly spaced square windows. Penthouse floors are set far back, capped by a low copper roof. Thus the scale is compatible with Burnham's buildings.

Around back, facing a neighborhood of low-scale residential and commercial buildings, the facades are "modern." Upper floors are set back with terraces behind a two-story screen, and the long facade is broken by a deep inset at the entrance. However, even these facades carry over the classical banding and rhythms found on the front.

The atrium offers a major counterstatement. Between blocklike entrance pavilions is a sheer glass entrance wall, and beyond this a high-tech glass interior. A steel spaceframe with a butt-glazed roof spans the 114-foot-square court. The walls are glass with fritted stripes to soften the light in the office space beyond. Towering clumps of bamboo provide shaded seating areas. This illusory space, all reflections and dappled light, is quite the opposite of the exterior homage to Burnham.

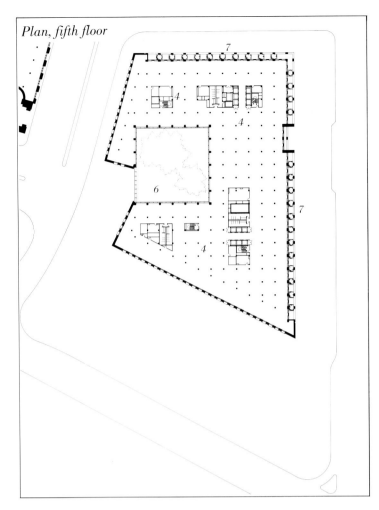

Plan, fifth floor

7

4

4

6

7

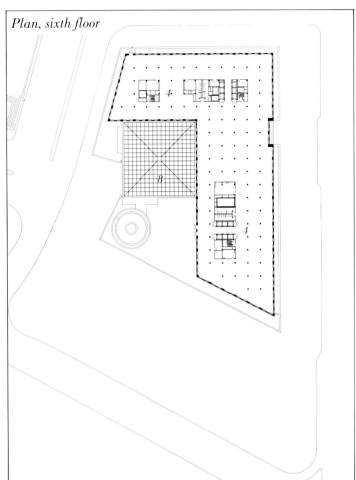

Plan, sixth floor

4

8

4

Plan, street level

F STREET

5   5

4

5

COLUMBUS CIRCLE

1   2

3   1

SECOND STREET

4

3   4

1

0   50   100   150 ft

MASSACHUSETTS AVENUE

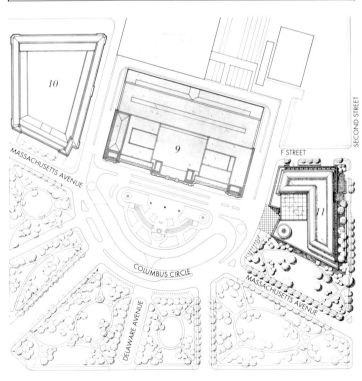

10

9

MASSACHUSETTS AVENUE

F STREET

SECOND STREET

11

COLUMBUS CIRCLE

DELAWARE AVENUE

MASSACHUSETTS AVENUE

0   200   400 ft

Cathedral of the Immaculate Conception

Burlington, Vermont, 1974–1977

Overleaf: View from the southwest.

The cathedral stands in a grove of honey-locusts. A green-brown copper roof rises up above the trees. The walls are shiny glazed brick, bands of dark brown and green. Radiating brick bands frame arched windows. David Wilson designed the stained glass.

One can enter the cathedral from any of three directions. A generous narthex and cross aisle are surrounded by vestry, sacristy, offices, and meeting rooms. The sanctuary is in a severe, lofty white room. Daylight comes from low arching windows, from a skylight above, and from a dark blue glass cross by Robert Sowers set deep into the thick entrance wall. Seating is in the round. Behind the organ is a small chapel. The marble baptismal font is by Mary Barnes; the tabernacle, by Alistair Bevington.

1 *Narthex and cross aisle*
2 *Chancel*
3 *Organ*
4 *St. Patrick's Chapel*
5 *Baptismal font*
6 *Tabernacle*
7 *Confessional*
8 *Vestry*
9 *Library*
10 *Sacristy*
11 *Office*
12 *Choir rehearsal room*
13 *Meeting room*
14 *Down to multipurpose room*

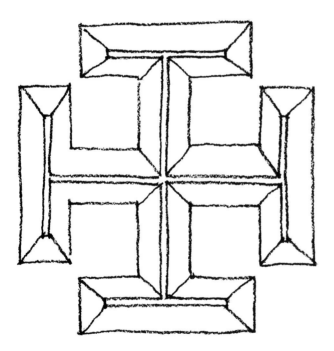

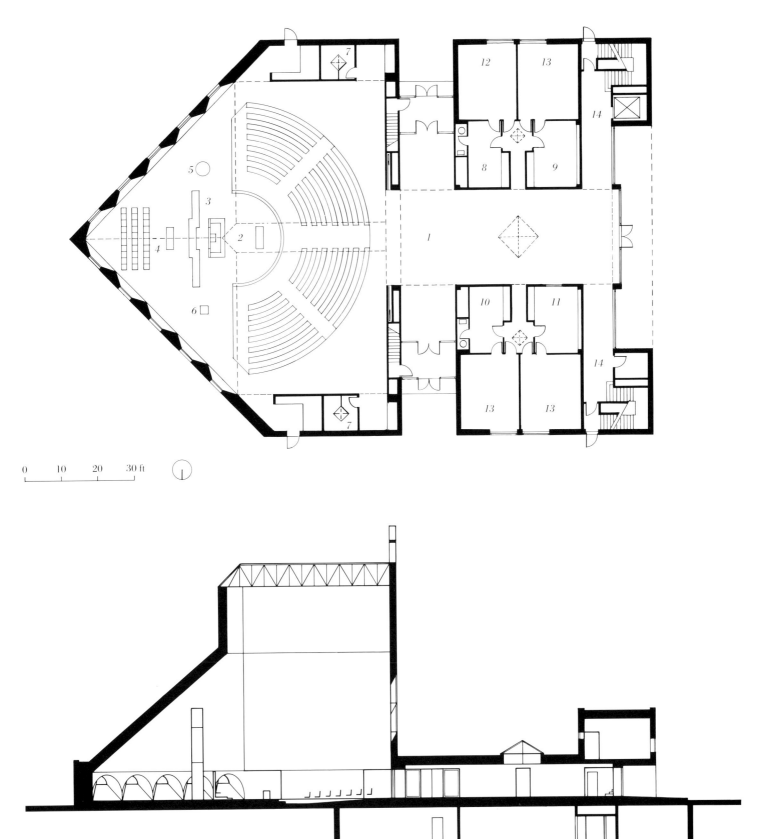

0 10 20 30 ft

Opposite: The altar, organ, pulpit, tabernacle, and baptismal font in the sanctuary.

Below: The sanctuary looking toward the narthex, with stained-glass cross by Robert Sowers.

Bottom: The baptismal font in front of stained-glass windows by David Wilson.

Overleaf: View from the northeast with cathedral roof and bell tower seen through the honey-locust grove.

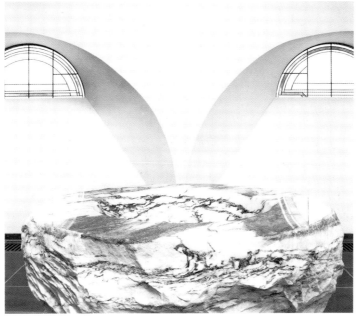

Sweeney Chapel, Christian Theological Seminary

Indianapolis, Indiana, 1984–1987

The chapel is the culmination of our master plan started twenty-five years before (see page 134). It stands at the corner of the academic court overlooking the White River, with the bell tower rising ninety feet.

The material, like the rest of the campus buildings, is cream-colored pebble concrete. Monumental doors facing the quadrangle are used only on ceremonial occasions, such as commencement. Daily entrance is from the corner of the cloister below the bell tower. Open stairs lead up to the balcony and tower or down to a choir rehearsal room overlooking the river.

The sanctuary is a cubic white volume with nothing but a cross, a table, a great organ, and mysterious light. There are two side windows looking out to woods and a window out of sight high above the altar. James Carpenter designed the side windows. Perpendicular to the window planes are vertical fins of clear glass and horizontal fins of dichroic glass, which splits the spectrum. As light passes through these "egg crate" windows, blue-green light reflects down and red-yellow light reflects up. As the sun moves, the colors and angles of the light passing through the dichroic glass continuously change. This simple effect in an otherwise spare room is very moving.

To one side is an arched opening and an alcove with a baptismal pool and a skylight. A bench along the wall provides a place for private thought.

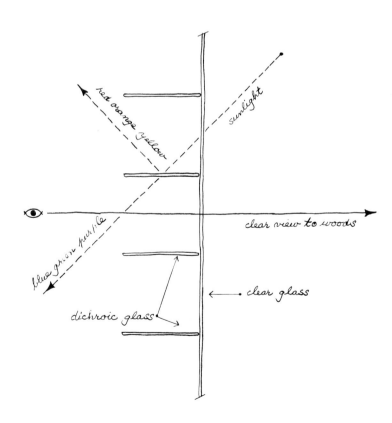

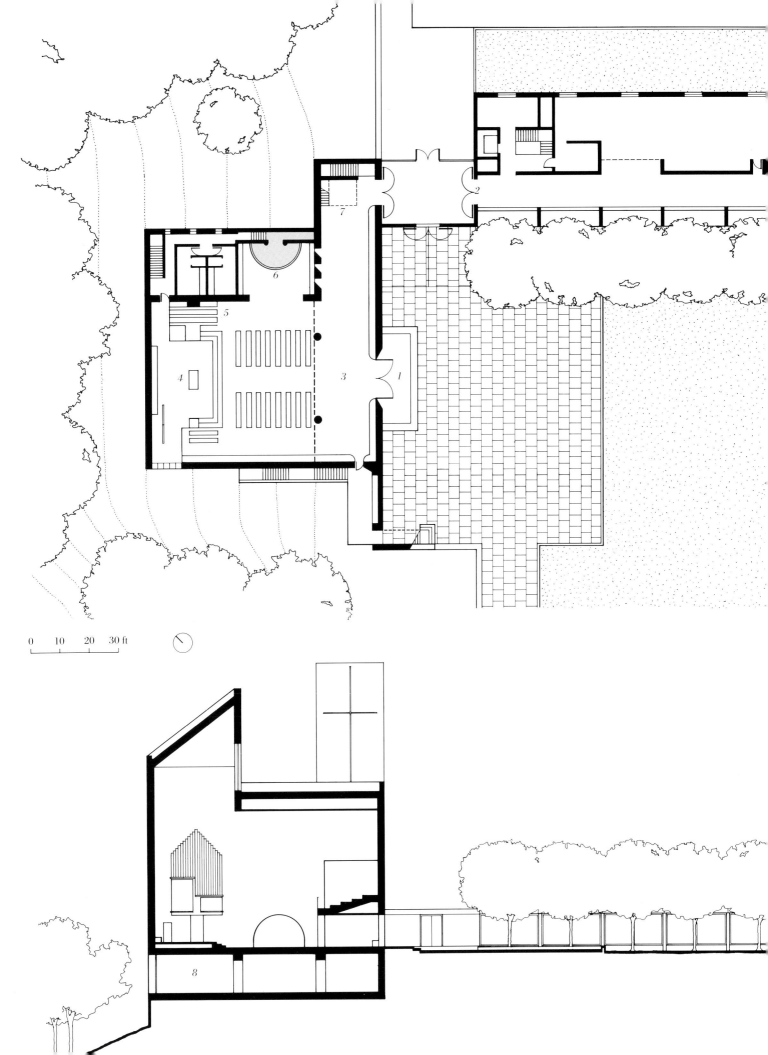

0 10 20 30 ft

Below: Bell-tower stairs, with balcony beyond.

Below: Baptistery pool.

*Below: Sanctuary with altar,
organ, and arched entrance
to baptistery.*

Walker Art Center

Minneapolis, Minnesota, 1966–1971, addition 1984

Seven galleries and three roof terraces step up around
the elevator core, from the entrance lobby to the rooftop
restaurant; they provide a sequential path through the
museum. One can follow the route up or down. Direct
access to individual galleries is also possible via the
elevator or core stairs, and individual galleries can be
closed for work without blocking circulation.

The galleries are basically neutral spaces, yet
continuously vary in proportion. Ceiling heights
increase from eleven to eighteen feet. One gallery
has a baffled window overlooking the park and a
broad balcony looking down to the lobby; another
has a skylight; and another a glass wall overlooking
a sculpture terrace. The gentle steps from gallery
to gallery present continually changing vistas that
alleviate museum fatigue and give each space
an identity.

At the top of the helical plan, a gallery opens to the
roof and three terraced outdoor galleries. The walls and
roof paving are all one material—a dark plum-colored
brick. Sculpture may be viewed from above or below,
against continuous pavements and high walls, or against
the Minneapolis skyline.

This quiet architecture does not compete with the art.
Flow, rather than form, was the concern.

In 1984, after these photographs were taken, we
expanded the administrative offices to the rear and
added subterranean galleries beneath stepped terraces
at the base of the building—a counterpoint to the
roof terraces in the original design.

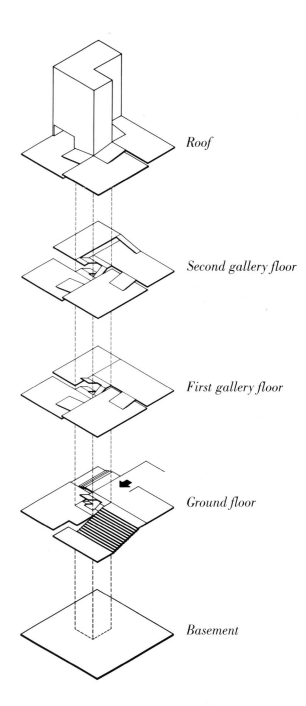

Roof

Second gallery floor

First gallery floor

Ground floor

Basement

1 Entrance
2 Guthrie Theater lobby
3 Walker Art Center lobby
4 Bookstore
5 Auditorium
6 Education studio

7 Lecture/information room
8 Gallery
9 Administration
10 Sculpture terrace
11 Restaurant

Plan, ground floor

Plan, second gallery floor

Plan, roof

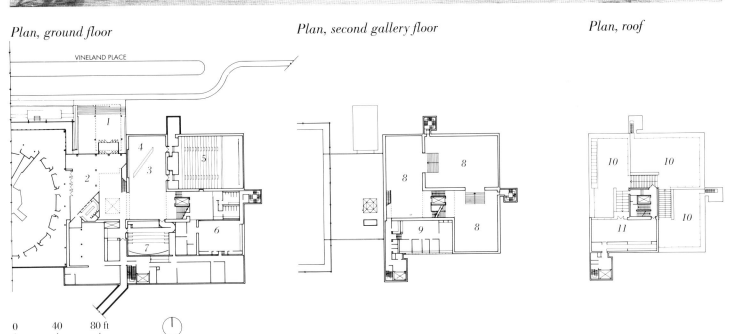

0   40   80 ft

Minneapolis Sculpture Garden

Minneapolis, Minnesota, 1986–1988

Sculpture gardens are too often a jumble of competing forms in open space—irrelevant relationships pitting one artist against another. What is needed is separation, clear background: outdoor *galleries* as distinct as indoor ones.

In 1985 the land across the street from the Walker Art Center became available, and we designed a formal axial garden with four terraced "galleries"—one-hundred-foot-square rooms framed by arborvitae hedges.

Two axes cross: one, from the Walker, focuses on a very large Claes Oldenburg–Coosje van Bruggen sculpture sitting in a pond. The other focuses on a greenhouse by Alistair Bevington that flanks one side of the garden. A bridge by Siah Armajani leads across an expressway from a city park. The museum overlooks all.

This garden combines focused containment and long vistas. One hopes that as the hedges grow tighter and taller, the composition will continue to improve—in time evoking the Tivoli Gardens in Italy.

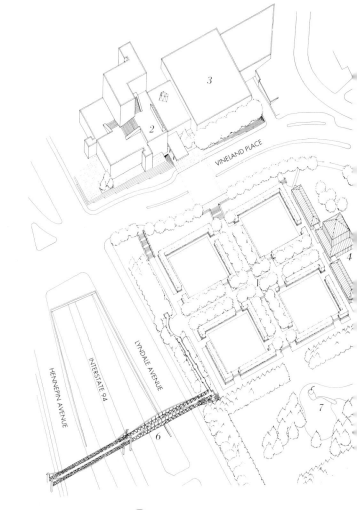

0   60   120   180 ft

1 Minneapolis Sculpture Garden
2 Walker Art Center
3 Guthrie Theater
4 Sage and John Cowles Conservatory
5 Service greenhouse
6 Irene Hixon Whitney Bridge (Siah Armajani)
7 Spoonbridge and Cherry (Claes Oldenburg and Coosje van Bruggen)
8 Parking

Sarah Scaife Gallery, The Carnegie Museum of Art

Pittsburgh, Pennsylvania, 1971–1974

On one hand the Scaife Gallery harmoniously extends the Carnegie Museum of Art. Scale and stone tie the two buildings together. On the other hand Scaife has its own identity, its own style.

A monumental Richard Serra sculpture stands in the entrance plaza. The glass entrance wall is under an overhang behind a line of water jets. Inside, a sidewalk café, a bookstore, temporary display areas, an auditorium, and other facilities cluster around a great sculpture courtyard that looks back to the Carnegie. A flight of steps leads gradually up along a forty-foot-high glass wall on one side of the courtyard to the gallery floor above.

The galleries are serene white spaces with skylights. Unlike traditional galleries with overhead skylights, here the light is deflected by a dropped ceiling and directed at the walls. The brightest surfaces are the walls, followed by the white terrazzo floors, and finally the ceilings. Incandescent light is carefully modulated for accent and support. The result is a glowing space darkening toward evening and changing from warm to cool with passing clouds.

The Scaife collection of impressionist paintings responds particularly well to changing light.

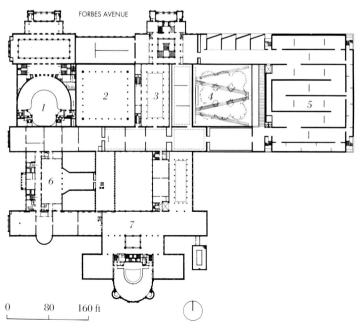

FORBES AVENUE

0   80   160 ft

Plan, second floor

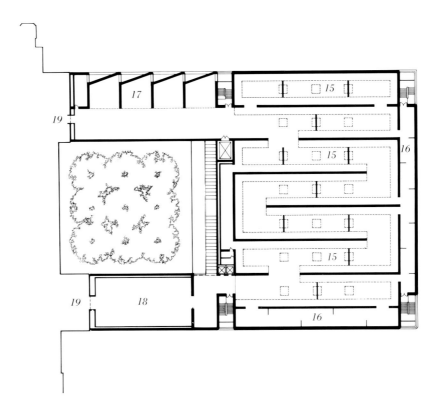

Plan, first floor

FORBES AVENUE

SOUTH CRAIG STREET

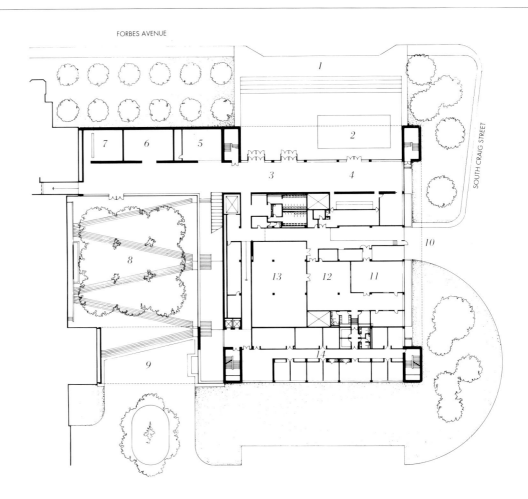

0   40   80 ft

Top photographs: Views of the sculpture courtyard through glass wall.

Above: View from Forbes Avenue.

Right: Dropped ceilings in the galleries deflect daylight onto the walls.

Dallas Museum of Art

Dallas, Texas, 1978–1983, additions 1984 and 1993

In the late 1970s the City of Dallas dedicated more than a dozen downtown blocks for an arts district. The Dallas Museum of Art was given a focal site at the end of a tree-lined street.

The museum was designed for modular growth. The initial phase (195,000 square feet) was completed in 1983. A small addition, the Reves Wing, was added almost at once. Then, in 1993, the Hamon Wing (100,000 square feet) was added with a seven-level underground parking garage.

The museum has a pedestrian entrance from the south, an automobile entrance from the north, and a ceremonial entrance in between. A "spine" hallway, gently sloping to the north down the site, connects the three entrances and provides access to various museum functions: bookstore, temporary gallery, auditorium, and restaurant. Each of these spaces can be opened or closed according to its own schedule, like shops along a street. At the north end is a reception hall with grand stairs and elevators leading up to permanent galleries and down to parking.

The galleries of the permanent collection, arranged on four trays stepping up to the north, set the tone for the whole museum. The terracing gives coherence to diverse collections. Each terrace has an internal garden court and skylights illuminating the outer walls. The lowest gallery, opposite the ceremonial entrance and opening on the sculpture garden, is dedicated to contemporary art. A huge Claes Oldenburg sculpture, *Stake Hitch*, dominates this vaulted room.

The sculpture garden, subdivided with limestone screens, waterwalls, and lush planting, allows each individual sculpture a sense of place.

The modular design not only accommodates expansion but breaks down the scale of what would be an enormous museum block. The form alternately advances and recedes, resulting in semi-enclosed outdoor courts, bold breaks in massing, and considerable interlock between open and closed spaces. The entire complex, including garden courts and barrel vault, is clad in Indiana limestone—a quiet continuous background for landscape as well as sculpture.

1 *Entrance*
2 *Sculpture garden*
3 *Sculpture garden (Richard Fleischner)*
4 *Vaulted gallery*
5 *Gallery*
6 *Open court*
7 *Reves Gallery*
8 *Three-story reception hall*
9 *Service entrance*
10 *Ramp down to parking garden*

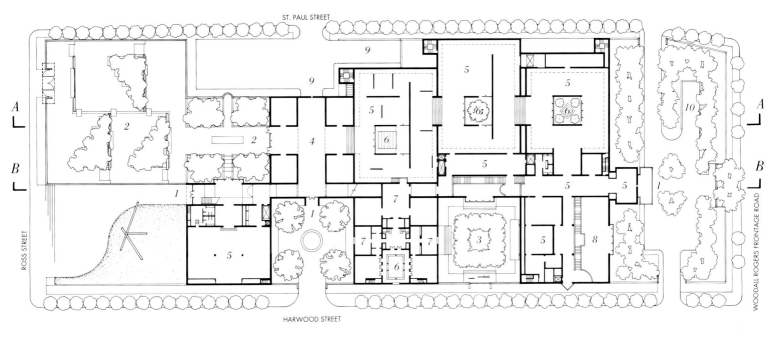

ST. PAUL STREET

ROSS STREET

HARWOOD STREET

WOODALL ROGERS FRONTAGE ROAD

Section AA through stepped galleries

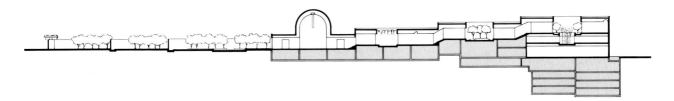

Section BB along spine

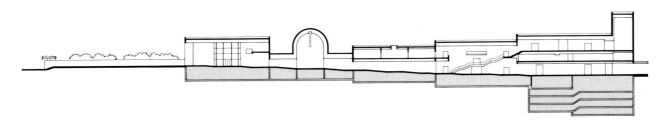

0   50   100 ft

*Below: The service entrance
on the west. The limestone
cladding is continuous on the
walls and roof.*

Below: An internal garden court.

Bottom: Gallery.

Opposite: The central vaulted gallery with Stake Hitch *by Claes Oldenburg. (The nail point of the sculpture emerges in the loading dock below.)*

Opposite: Limestone screens in the sculpture garden.

Below: Barrel vault seen from the sculpture garden.

Bottom: Ceremonial entrance on the east.

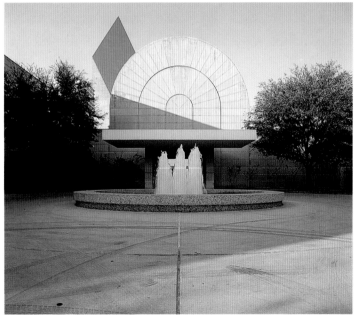

Chicago Botanic Garden

Glencoe, Illinois, 1970–1976
Visitors Center, 1993

*Overleaf: Central exhibition
hall and greenhouses.*

Since the 1960s the Chicago Botanic Garden has
transformed marshland into a picturesque landscape
of garden islands and meandering lagoons. In 1970
we were commissioned to design an education/
administration center on the main island. Much later,
in 1990, we were asked to design a gateway building
for visitors just off the island near the parking lot.

From the parking lot or bus stop, one comes to the
visitors center, a low brick building at the water's edge.
A high brick hall leads straight through the building to
a bridge to the main island. The hall has a garden shop
on the right and a café on the left; both have tent roofs,
skylights, and decks cantilevered out over the water and
shaded by enormous willow trees. Across the lagoon one
can see island flower gardens reflected in water.

A wooden suspension bridge takes one to the island and
the education/administration building. Like the visitors
center, this structure has a strong cruciform plan, a
sense of containment. Such formality seemed desirable
as a foil to the random picturesqueness of the island
planting. A central hall straight through the building
passes two cloistered courts, one with a forty-nine-jet
fountain. A cross hall looks out between administrative
offices and auditorium to lawns and water.

The focus of the composition is a great pyramidal
exhibition hall surrounded by a cluster of ten
greenhouses. The greenhouses are square pavilions
suitable for the display of separate climate biomes. The
central exhibition hall, with a strip hemlock ceiling,
low windows to the courtyards, and a high roof monitor
bringing in streaks of light, is truly a commanding
space. The copper roof announces the center of the
320-acre garden park.

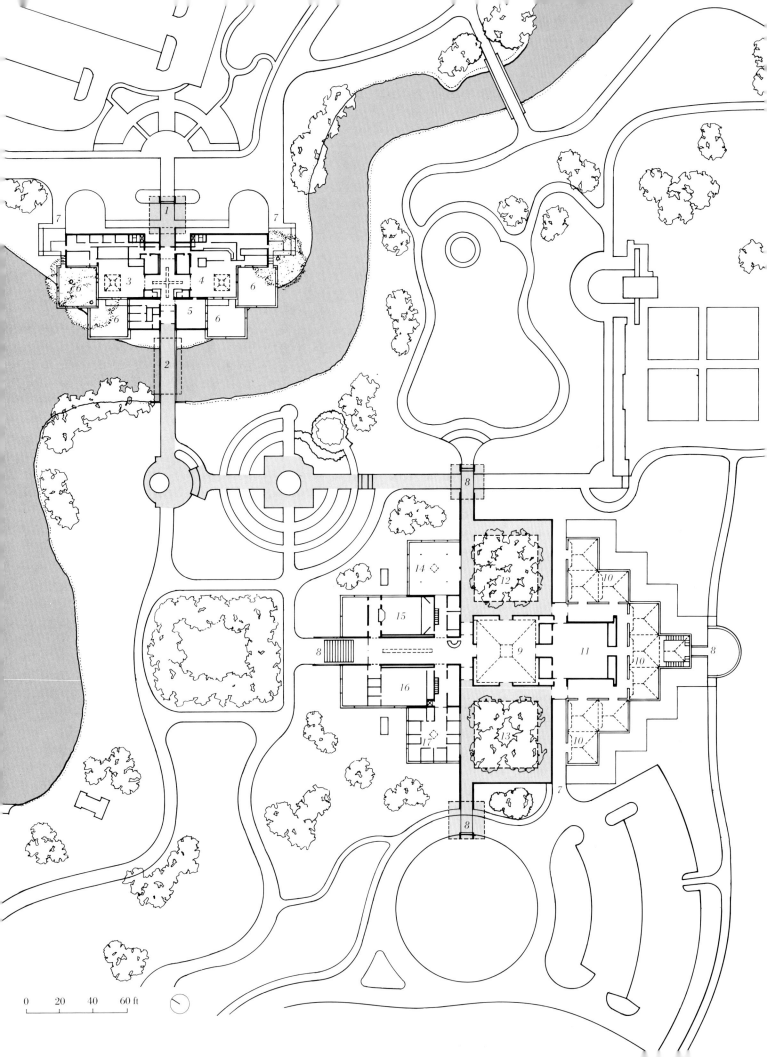

1 2 3 4 5 6 7

8

8

14

15 16 17

12 9 10 11 10 13 7 10

0   20   40   60 ft

Below: North entrance to exhibition hall.

Bottom: Fountain court.

Opposite: Pyramidal roof of exhibition hall with open-strip hemlock ceiling.

*Below: Willows hang over a
visitors center deck.*

*Bottom: This bridge leads
from the visitors center to the
education/administration
building.*

*Opposite and below: The
entrance to the visitors center.*   *Bottom: The central hall in
the visitors center.*

Chronology

Chronology

1915
Born in Chicago, Illinois

1938
B.S. *cum laude*, Harvard College

1941–1942
Sheldon Traveling Fellowship

1942
M.Arch., Harvard University

1946

Prefabricated House
Consolidated Vultee Aircraft
Corporation
California, 1947
Henry Dreyfuss, Designer;
Edward Larrabee Barnes, Architect

See page 16

1948

Reid House
Purchase, New York, 1950
My first house, a dream job for a young
architect. It is what my teacher Marcel
Breuer called a binuclear house: a stair
hall separates the living room and
library from the rest of the house. The
materials are fieldstone inside and out,
cypress siding, and white plaster.

1949

Osborn House
Salisbury, Connecticut, 1950
Studio, 1951

See page 22

1950

Buck House
Lakeville, Connecticut, 1952

See page 22

John Marin Room
Downtown Gallery
New York, New York, 1950

O'Connell House
Alpine, New Jersey, 1951
Another binuclear house. Again, the
link is the staircase. From the carport
and front hall one ascends to a dining-
bedroom wing with garden terrace
behind. One then crosses back over a
bridge to a living room on stilts with an
open porch overlooking the valley.

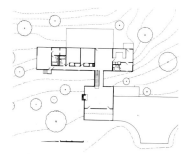

Weiner House
Fort Worth, Texas, 1952
The roof is supported on exposed steel
columns. The stone walls are simply
screens. The result is a free-flowing
space in which front hall, living room,
family room, dining room, and veranda
are all one. The rest of the house—the
bedrooms, service wing, playhouse,
etc.—is contained in crisp white boxes.

1951

Barnes House *See page 22*
Mount Kisco, New York, 1952, 1971, 1975
The original platform house is in the center. Twenty years later a studio apartment was added to the west (left) and then a master bedroom with office below to the east (right). Floor levels follow the sloping terrain. Roofs angle sharply. Thus the additions are a foil to the original classic design.

1952

Marsters House
Litchfield, Connecticut, 1955

See page 22

United Lodge of Theosophists Remodeling
New York, New York, 1954

1953

Mercedes-Benz Showroom
New York, New York

Fresh Air Fund Camps *See page 78*
Sharpe Reservation, Fishkill, New York
Camp Bliss, 1955
Camp Anita, 1955
Camp Hayden, 1960
Richard Moger
Camp Hidden Valley, 1961
Noel Yauch
Over several years we built a succession of camps for disadvantaged children, all sponsored by the *New York Herald Tribune*. At Camp Hayden the dining and village halls are stone—enormous boulders, with battered walls and beams supported on trees. At Camp Bliss the construction is lighter—dining and village halls have triangular windows at the ends, screened openings along the sides, and balanced lightweight trusses. Tent platforms make it possible to camp in rough terrain.

1954
Design Critic and Lecturer, Pratt Institute (until 1959)

1955

Pan American Airlines Corporate Identity Program
1960
With Charles Forberg
The original commission was for ticket offices and jet plane interiors. We soon convinced Pan Am to expand the project to include a whole new "look"—logo, color scheme, and trademark. (The *New York Times* recently reported that this logo and trademark are up for sale for over $1,325,000!)

1956

Miller House
Chappaqua, New York, 1957
In woods on a hillside, this post-and-beam structure has coffee-colored siding and blue-green glass between the beams and in the peaked windows.

1956

Straus House
Pound Ridge, New York, 1958
Norman Lebowitz

See page 28

1957
Design Critic and Lecturer,
Yale University (until 1964)

Capitol Towers Apartments
Sacramento, California, 1960
Wurster, Bernardi and Emmons; DeMars
and Reay, Associate Architects

See page 18

WVIP Radio Station
Mount Kisco, New York, 1958
Howard Battin, Associate Architects
A spiral plan with ascending ceiling.
The control room is in the center
surrounded by wedge-shaped studios.
A reception room looks out to a glass
entrance wall. Here I did a full height
photomural of my son listening to a
conch shell.

1958

**Haystack Mountain School of
Crafts**
Deer Isle, Maine, 1961, 1979
Giovanni Pasanella, 1961
Hildegarde Bergeim, 1979

See page 70

El Monte Apartments
San Juan, Puerto Rico, 1961, 1967
Joseph Merz; Reed, Basora and
Menendez, Associate Architects

See page 18

United States Consulate
Tabriz, Iran, 1966
Gus Rohrs
A walled compound of load-bearing
brick stuccoed white. The consulate
office (far right) has brick arches that
support domes one brick thick, laid in
rings without formwork. Buttresses resist
earthquake forces. The consul's
residence (right) combines brick domes
with barrel vaults.

1959
A. W. Brunner Prize, National
Institute of Arts and Letters

Yale University Award for
Distinction in the Arts

Henry Kaufmann Campgrounds
Wyandanch, New York, 1961
Richard Moger, Assoc.
On a wooded slope on Long Island these
three circular pools (deep, medium, and
shallow) step down the hill on nesting
eye-shaped terraces. Changing rooms,
open to the sky, extend from each end.

Jack Lenor Larsen Showroom
New York, New York, 1960
With Charles Forberg

Dormitories
St. Paul's School, Concord, New
Hampshire, 1962
Richard Moger, Assoc.; Giovanni
Pasanella, Alistair Bevington

See page 82

Cowles House
Wayzata, Minnesota, 1962
Hildegarde Bergeim, Proj. Arch.

See page 34

1960
Silver Medal for the Straus House,
Architectural League of New York

Director, Municipal Art Society
of New York

Menotti/Barber Studios
Mount Kisco, New York, 1962
Giovanni Pasanella, Proj. Arch.

Ford Foundation Theater
Project
With Jo Mielziner, theater designer
A one-thousand-seat theater designed
for *intimate* opera. The acoustic ceiling
covers audience, pit, and thrust stage.
Scenic support is possible in the center,
at the sides, or all the way across. The
exterior form, two truncated cones
tipped toward each other, expresses
conical sight lines, the sweep of the
stage, and the scenery lifting heights.

 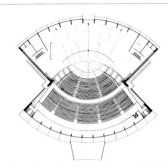

**Roosevelt Memorial
Competition**
Washington, D.C.
*With Jaquelin Robertson and Giovanni
Pasanella*
A calm, reflective memorial for Franklin
Delano Roosevelt. A great lawn slopes
up to a walk that looks across to the
Washington, Jefferson, and Lincoln
memorials. Along the walk are a grove of
trees, benches for contemplation, and
plaques with quotations from Roosevelt.

1961
Treasurer, Municipal Art Society
of New York

**Helen Newberry Joy
Residence for Women**
*Wayne State University, Detroit,
Michigan, 1964*
*Richard Moger, Assoc.; Giovanni
Pasanella, Proj. Arch.; Hildegarde Bergeim*
In a campus surrounded by parking and
service roads, this dormitory looks out
on a great lawn sloping up to an
enclosing wall. The result is a calm
outdoor space, a sense of sky, and an
escape from the urban environment.

**Neiman Marcus Shopping
Center**
Fort Worth, Texas, 1963
Stanley Maurer, Proj. Arch.
Neiman Marcus stands on sloping
ground with shops stepping down around
each side. Access to Neiman Marcus is
from the ends through little courtyards.
Access to the shops is directly from the
parking lot or from Neiman Marcus.
The material is white stucco with white-
on-white signage.

Christian Theological Seminary

See pages 134 and 190

Indianapolis, Indiana
Master Planner, 1961–1987
Greek Theater, Classroom and Administration Building, 1966
Richard Moger, Hildegarde Bergeim, Assocs.; Gus Rohrs, Proj. Arch.
Library, 1977
Hildegarde Bergeim, Assoc.; Gajinder Singh, Proj. Arch.
Student Housing, 1986
Mark Cavagnero, Proj. Arch.
Sweeney Chapel, 1987
Robert Junk, Proj. Arch.

Freshman Dean's House

Yale University, New Haven,
Connecticut, Project
Giovanni Pasanella, Proj. Arch.
We proposed this house for the freshman
dean for a corner of the old campus
surrounded by brownstone buildings. It
was a four-story tower: a low entrance
with garage, a high-ceilinged parlor,
bedrooms, and a family room with
peaked roof and terrace. The material
is all brownstone, including the roof.

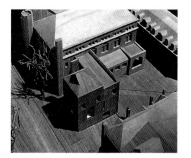

State University of New York at Potsdam

See page 118

Stanley Maurer, Assoc.
Hildegarde Bergeim, John Copelin, Ira Goldfarb, Albert Henriques, Percy Keck,
Judy Klein, William Lee, Martin McNeill, Marvin Mitchell, Giovanni Pasanella,
Mildred Popkin, Gus Rohrs, Evan Schwartz, Gajinder Singh, Siglinde Stern,
Frank Tomaino
Master Planner, 1962–1970; Dormitory, 1966;
Library, 1967; Classroom Building, 1967;
Lecture Halls, 1968; Dormitory, 1970;
Fine Arts Building, 1970; Student Union, 1970;
Crane Music Center, 1973

Henry House

Blue Mountain Lake, New York, Project
Noel Yauch, Proj. Arch.
A lakeside house. One enters under a
cantilever to ascend a few steps to the
living room. A few more steps lead to the
dining room–kitchen, then up past the
guest room to the master bedroom. From
there, one can exit to the roof and
continue on up around the core to the
uppermost roof. Note the similarity to
the Walker Art Center plan on page 198.

Henry House

Blue Mountain Lake, New York, 1964
Noel Yauch, Proj. Arch.
The first scheme was never built—too
many steps. We designed the second
scheme from the opposite point of view.
This house is built into the hill like an
Adirondack lean-to. One enters through
a dormer in the roof and descends into a
high-ceilinged living room overlooking
the lake.

Administration Building

Princeton University, New Jersey, 1965
Alistair Bevington, Assoc.
A poured concrete, "clean modern"
building on the edge of a collegiate
Gothic campus. Compare the contextual
Allen Library, done thirty years later
(see page 114). Which is right? Were we
insensitive in 1962? Are we chameleons
now? Architecture must be part of the
fabric and *also* stand alone.

Dormitories

Rochester Institute of Technology, New
York, 1967
Gus Rohrs, Proj. Arch.
In 1962 we collaborated with Dan Kiley,
Lawrence Anderson, Kevin Roche,
Hugh Stubbins, and Harry Weese on a
campus plan for R.I.T. Our student
housing complex stands on a rise facing
the academic campus. The massing
ascends from low dormitories through
courtyards to high-rise blocks.

 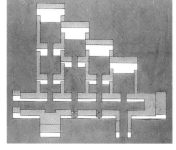

1963

Merit Award for Capitol Towers
Apartments, AIA Northern California
and East Bay Chapters

First Honor Award for El Monte
Apartments, United States Federal
Housing Administration

Trustee, American Academy in Rome
(until 1978)

Andrew Rockefeller House
Greenwich, Connecticut, 1965
Hildegarde Bergeim, Assoc.
This three-story house steps down a
wooded hillside. Peaked roofs bring
sunlight to rooms below.

**W. D. Richards Elementary
School**
Columbus, Indiana, 1965
*Richard Moger, Assoc.; Jaquelin
Robertson, Proj. Arch.*
The school, with courts and terraces,
floats on a platform. The factorylike
sawtooth roof brings top light to *every*
room—to the gymnasium and cafeteria
and all surrounding classrooms.

Righter House
Fishers Island, New York, 1965
Siglinde Stern, Proj. Arch.

See page 42

Emma Willard School
Troy, New York
Noel Yauch, Assoc.
Master Planner, 1963–1971
Faculty Apartments, 1966
Library, Music, and Art Building, 1967,
1971

See pages 90 and 96

**New England Merchants
National Bank**
Boston, Massachusetts, 1970
Alistair Bevington, Robert Siegel, Assocs.

See page 142

1964

First Honor Awards for El Monte
Apartments and Capitol Towers
Apartments, United States Urban
Renewal Administration

1965

Citation in Landscape Architecture for
Haystack Mountain School of Crafts,
Architectural League of New York

Visiting Committee, Massachusetts
Institute of Technology (until 1968)

Pratt Institute Master Plan
Brooklyn, New York
Alistair Bevington, Assoc.

Wye Institute
Cheston-on-Wye, Maryland, 1968
Jaquelin Robertson, Proj. Arch.
A summer camp on the Wye River in
Maryland. A broad central walkway
extends 576 feet straight from parking
lot to riverfront. Indoor activities are
south of the walk, athletics on the north.
The buildings have shingle-covered
shed roofs.

1965

Guest House
John D. Rockefeller III
Tarrytown, New York, 1967
George Large, Proj. Arch.
A dark-stained house in the woods with peaked roofs and triangular windows looking up to the trees. The windows have rolling, sail-like shades.

Dormitories
Bennington College, Vermont, 1967
Charles Gwathmey, Proj. Arch.
White dormitories, like farm buildings, back up a line of older colonial houses. Flat roofs over the bedrooms are offset by steeply raking roofs over stairs and lounges.

Student Union, Theater, and Amphitheater
Monterey Peninsula Junior College, California, 1970
Alexander Cooper, Jr., Proj. Arch.; Keeble and Rhoda; Douglas Barker, Associate Architects
The campus is bisected by a ravine. The student union and theater are at its head with the amphitheater between them. The ravine is now an artery and the amphitheater a campus center.

 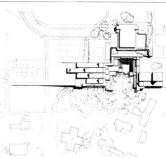

1966
Fellow, American Institute of Architects

Hooker State School
New Haven, Connecticut, 1975
John Lee, Assoc.; Martin Rich, Proj. Arch.

Walker Art Center
Minneapolis, Minnesota, 1971, 1984
Alistair Bevington, Assoc.; Justin Lamb, Martin Rich, Proj. Archs., 1971
Hildegarde Bergeim, Alistair Bevington, Assocs., 1984

See page 198

State University of New York at Purchase
Stanley Maurer, Arthur Baker, Richard Balser, Assocs.
Master Planner, 1966–1977;
Gymnasium, 1972, *Roger Clarke, Proj. Arch.*
Student Activities Building A, 1972, *John Hagmann, Proj. Arch.*
Student Activities Building B, 1972
Library, 1973, *Hildegarde Bergeim, Michael Wurmfeld, Assocs.*
Performing Arts Center, 1977, *Bruce Fowle, Arthur Baker, Assocs.*
Music Instruction Building, 1977, *Rolf Karl, Assoc.*

See page 122

University of Chicago
Chicago, Illinois
Master Plan
Robert Siegel, Noel Yauch, Percy Keck, Michael Wurmfeld, Assocs.
Smart Gallery, 1974
Percy Keck, Assoc.; Bal Baswant
The plan encompassed an arts center, student housing, and a gymnasium. The layout provided clear entrances, vistas, defined courts, and varied roof lines. The Smart Gallery is at the east end.

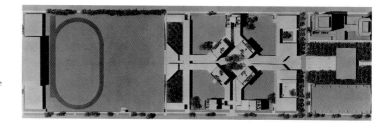

1967
Member, Westchester
Council of the Arts (until 1971)

Crown Center
Kansas City, Missouri
Marshall & Brown, Associate Architects
Master Planner, 1967–1982
Office Complex, 1972
Retail Building, 1972
John Lee, Edward Jacobson, Assocs.
Hallmark Garage, 1980
Edward Jacobson, Assoc.
Hallmark Headquarters, 1982
Michael Timchula, Assoc.

See page 146

Yale University
New Haven, Connecticut
Master Planner, 1968–1978
Cross Campus Library, 1971
John Lee, Assoc.; Herbert Goldberg, Proj. Arch.
Farnam and Vanderbilt Halls Renovation, 1976
Edward Jacobson, Assoc.; Thomas Czarnowski, Frederick Stelle, Proj. Archs.
School of Organization and Management, 1978
Edward Jacobson, Assoc.; Thomas Czarnowski, Proj. Arch.
Smilow Field House Renovation and Addition, 1993
John Lee, Partner; Daniel Casey, Assoc.; Richard Klibschon, Proj. Arch.
High and Wall Streets Pedestrian Walk, 1993
Steven Fisher, Assoc.; Richard Klibschon, Proj. Arch.
Henry R. Luce Hall, Yale Center for International and Area Studies, 1995
Alistair Bevington, Partner; Joseph Weiss, Richard Klibschon, Proj. Archs.
Since 1967 our work at Yale has been varied: master planning; underground expansion of the Sterling Memorial Library; renovation of historic nineteenth-century dormitories; creation of a business school by combining two historic mansions, a modern computer center, and a small observatory around a sunken grassy court (top right); expansion of a field house; designs for closing inner-campus streets; and now a new building—the Henry R. Luce Hall for International and Area Studies (bottom right).

St. Paul's School
Concord, New Hampshire
Kittredge Dormitory, 1970
Alistair Bevington, Assoc.
Tuck Shop, 1970
Siglinde Stern, Proj. Arch.
A central spine hall runs from the street to the pond. Clustered on each side are three dormitories with sleeping alcoves for younger boys overlooked by apartments for single masters. At each end are townhouses for married masters.

1969
Associate, National Academy of Design

Rockefeller Hall
Harvard University Divinity School,
Cambridge, Massachusetts, 1971
Edward Jacobson, John Lee, Percy Keck,
Assocs.
On a tight site, this little dormitory is built as a tower with thirteen beds to a floor. The lounge, meeting rooms, and dining rooms spread out on the first floor with high ceilings and large windows.

1970
"Architecture for the State University of New York at Purchase," The Katonah Gallery

Spring Hill Conference Center
Wayzata, Minnesota, 1972, 1985
Hildegarde Bergeim, Assoc., 1972
Siglinde Stern, Proj. Arch., 1985
Converting the Cowles House (page 34) to a conference center was not easy, but in the end the complex has great domestic charm. Bedrooms, barnlike meeting rooms, and dining rooms cluster around courts, while at the center, the former living room remains friendly and noninstitutional.

1970

Chicago Botanic Garden
Glencoe, Illinois, 1976, 1993
Alistair Bevington, Assoc.; Gajinder
Singh, Proj. Arch., 1976
Alistair Bevington, Partner; Siglinde
Stern, Proj. Arch., 1993

See page 222

1971
"Architecture for the Arts: State
University of New York at Purchase,"
Museum of Modern Art

Medal of Honor, AIA New York Chapter

Law School
Drake University, Des Moines, Iowa,
1974
John Lee, Assoc.; David Arnold, Daniel
Casey, Proj. Archs.

Righter House
Bedford Hills, New York, 1975
Laurie Maurer
An open plan for a couple with grown
children. The major rooms—the living
room, bedroom, library, dining room,
and kitchen—have sliding doorways to
allow an uninterrupted flow of space.
Staggered massing creates small outdoor
courts.

Heckscher House
Mount Desert Island, Maine, 1974
John Lee, Assoc.; Rolf Karl, Marvin
Mitchell, Proj. Archs.

See page 46

**Sarah Scaife Gallery,
The Carnegie Museum of Art**
Pittsburgh, Pennsylvania, 1974
Percy Keck, Assoc.; Armand Avakian,
Proj. Arch.

See page 210

1972
AIA Collaborative Achievement Award
for Rochester Institute of Technology

AIA Honor Award for Walker Art Center

Merit Award for A. Rockefeller House,
American Society of Landscape Architects

Harleston Parker Medal for the New
England Merchants National Bank,
Boston Society of Architects

Member, Urban Design Council of the
City of New York (until 1976)

American Savings Bank
Queens, New York, 1974
John Lee, Assoc.; Demetri Sarantitis,
Proj. Arch.
A small branch bank in Queens with an
angled entrance, a simple glass facade,
and a line of trees.

Visual Arts Center
Bowdoin College, Maine, 1976
Alistair Bevington, Assoc.; Demetri
Sarantitis, Proj. Arch.

See page 104

**Americas/Far East
Headquarters, IBM World
Trade Corporation**
Mount Pleasant, New York, 1975
John Lee, Bruce Fowle, Martin Rich,
Assocs.

See page 150

1973
First Vice President, American
Academy in Rome

Plants and Man Building
New York Botanical Garden, Project
Alistair Bevington, Assoc.; David Arnold,
Proj. Arch.
A cluster of hexagonal modules housing
worldwide climate zones. The organic
configuration is flexible. The hexagons
can be combined to make chambers of
any size or height. The complex can jog
to meet site conditions and can expand
horizontally by adding modules or
vertically by raising the roof.

Museum of Pueblo and Navaho Art

Santa Fe, New Mexico, Project
With Dr. Alfonso Ortiz
Pueblo life is agrarian, rooted, timeless, and centered on the kiva. This centripetal culture is displayed in the central circular gallery. Navaho life is restless, with periods of conquest, exile, and intermittent peace. This centrifugal culture is shown chronologically in spaces fluctuating between the square and the circle.

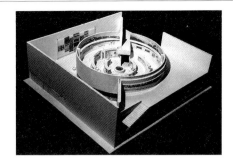

Music and Art Building

Colorado College, Colorado Springs, 1976
Edward Jacobson, Assoc.
An intimate concert hall with "ring" seating is linked by a skylit gallery to a studio/classroom tower. Studios are stacked vertically, four stories high, with stepped balconies looking out to the Rocky Mountains. The materials are white stucco accented with bold primary colors and black and white tile.

Chilmark Houses: McNamara, Meyer, Ginsburg

Martha's Vineyard, Massachusetts, 1975
Bruce Fowle, Assoc.; Laurie Maurer

IBM 590 Madison Avenue

New York, New York, 1983
John Lee, Partner; Armand Avakian, Assoc.; Richard Klibschon, Proj. Arch.

See page 158

Chappaqua, New York, Schools

John Lee, Assoc.
Robert E. Bell School Gymnasium, 1975
Richard Klibschon, Proj. Arch.
West Orchard Middle School Addition, 1980, *Daniel Quinn, Proj. Arch.*

1974
Academician, National Academy of Design

"Retrospective," Sarah Scaife Gallery

Cathedral of the Immaculate Conception

Burlington, Vermont, 1977
Alistair Bevington, Assoc.; Demetri Sarantitis, Proj. Arch.

See page 182

Wichita Art Museum Expansion

Wichita, Kansas, 1977
John Lee, Assoc.; Michael Timchula, Proj. Arch.; Platt Assocs., Associate Architects
The Wichita Museum, designed by Clarence Stein in 1928, had been badly remodeled. We stripped away the additions and built a new museum *around* the Stein block, creating a square within a square.

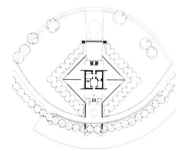

Main Gate and Conservatory Restoration

New York Botanical Garden, 1979
Alistair Bevington, Percy Keck, Assocs.; Siglinde Stern, Michael Timchula, Hillary Brown
The 1899 conservatory badly needed repair. Instead of substituting coarse aluminum window frames, we restored the original cast-iron detailing and added a new landscaped entrance and stone gateway wall on Southern Boulevard.

1974

Arts and Sciences Building
Miss Porter's School, Farmington,
Connecticut, 1976
John Lee, Assoc.; Gajinder Singh, Proj.
Arch.

1975
First Vice Chairman, American
Academy in Rome

Trustee, Museum of Modern Art (until
1992)

Garden Library   *See page 62*
Upperville, Virginia, 1983
Siglinde Stern, Proj. Arch.

1976
Member, Westchester Planning Board
(until 1988)

Indiana University   *See page 130*
Since 1976 we have worked for Indiana University on three campuses as planning
consultant and architect. In Indianapolis we have done some ten buildings, including
the Natatorium (top right). In South Bend we did a master plan with a 1,100-foot mall
to the river bluff, where we designed a small high-rise library (bottom right). A
classroom/office building and garage flanking the mall are now being designed. In
Bloomington we are completing a large undergraduate recreational sports facility for
swimming, diving, basketball, and court games.

Indiana University/Purdue University at Indianapolis
Gajinder Singh, Assoc.
Planning Consultant, 1976–1993
Two Garages, 1979
School of Business/School of Planning and Environmental Administration, 1980
John Lee, Assoc.
School of Education/School of Social Work, 1981
James Associates, Associate Architects
Natatorium, 1982
Browning Day Pollak Mullins, Associate Architects
Conference Center, 1987
Archonics, Associate Architects
Science, Engineering and Technology Building, 1991, 1993
Plus 4, Associate Architects
Blake Street Garage, 1992
Library, 1993
Jonathan Jaffe, Anne Wattenberg, Proj. Archs.; HNTB, Associate Architects
Fountain, 1994

Indiana University at South Bend
Gajinder Singh, Assoc.
Planning Consultant, 1985–1993
Library, 1988
John Lee, Partner; Anne Wattenberg, Richard Klibschon, Proj. Archs.
Garage, 1994
Afzaal Nasiruddeen, Proj. Arch.
Classroom/Office Building, 1995

Indiana University at Bloomington
Gajinder Singh, Assoc.
Planning Consultant, 1987
Garage, 1988
With Walker Parking Consultants
Recreational Sports Facility, 1995
Richard Ridge, Proj. Arch.; Browning Day Mullins Dierdorf, Associate Architects

Museum of Art
Fort Lauderdale, Florida, 1985
Michael Timchula, Assoc.; James
Fraerman, Proj. Arch.
Convex and concave stucco walls echo
the shape of the street. A central
breezeway leads to parking. On the left
(concave side) is an auditorium with a
sculpture terrace above. On the right
(convex side) is the museum. Inside, a
sweeping stair leads along a curved wall
to high-ceilinged galleries.

Utah State University
Logan, Utah
Art and Landscape Architecture Building, 1980
Bruce Fowle, Assoc.; Daniel Casey, Proj. Arch.; William F. Thomas, Associate Architects
Nora Eccles Harrison Museum of Art, 1982
Daniel Casey, Proj. Arch.; Thomas Petersen Hammond & Assoc., Associate Architects
Science and Technology Library, 1994; Space Dynamics Laboratory, 1994
John Lee, Partner; Steven Fisher, Assoc; Jensen, Haslem, Campbell & Hardcastle, Associate Architects
Work began with an arts center: studios and a museum linked to an existing theater around a brick court. More recently we designed a science library in the center of the main campus as well as a laboratory for an outlying research park.

General Academic Building
North Carolina State University, Raleigh, 1982
Edward Jacobson, Assoc.; J. N. Pease Assoc., Associate Architects

1977
AIA Honor Award for Heckscher House

Mobil Corporation Technical Center
Hopewell Township, New Jersey, 1990
Thomas Czarnowski, Daniel Casey, Assocs.
Master Planner and Architectural Consultant

1978
Merit Award for IBM World Trade Corporation, American Society of Landscape Architects

Albert S. Bard Award for Excellence in Architecture and Urban Design for the N.Y. Botanical Garden Restoration, City Club of New York

Fellow, American Academy of Arts and Sciences

Visiting Committee, Harvard University Graduate School of Design (until 1984)

Duke University
Durham, North Carolina
Fuqua School of Business, 1983
Edward Jacobson, Assoc.
Thomas Executive Education Center, 1989
Percy Keck, John Lee, Partners; Mark Cavagnero, Joseph Weiss, Proj. Archs.
The Fuqua School and the Thomas Center flank a wooded ravine and are connected by a covered bridge. Both have lecture, seminar, and dining rooms. The two facilities relate symbiotically.

Museum of Fine Arts Expansion
Museum of New Mexico, Santa Fe, 1983
Demetri Sarantitis, Proj. Arch.; Antoine Predock, Associate Architects

Dallas Museum of Art
Dallas, Texas, 1983, 1984, 1993
Alistair Bevington, John Lee, Partners; Daniel Casey, Proj. Arch., Siglinde Stern, 1983, 1984
Alistair Bevington, Partner; Uiko Zecha, Robert Hart, Proj. Archs., 1993

See page 214

1010 Market Street
St. Louis, Missouri, 1982
John Lee, Partner; Robert Segal, Proj. Arch.; Lien Chen
A twenty-story office building with broadcasting facilities for KSDK–TV. The tower, with landscaped plaza, anchors one end of the St. Louis Mall. The materials are light gray granite and green glass.

Asia Society Gallery
New York, New York, 1981
John Lee, Partner; Richard Ridge, Proj. Arch.
A strong facade on Park Avenue and a little terrace garden on the side street. Public spaces—auditorium, bookstore, and art galleries—are on lower floors. Offices are on middle floors. Conference rooms and boardrooms with sweeping arched windows are on top. The exterior is red granite with either a thermal or a polished finish; the interior features red sandstone from India on the lower floors, monumental stairs, and terrace paving.

1978

535 Madison Avenue
New York, New York, 1982
Percy Keck, Partner; Steven Fisher, Proj. Arch.
An office building should not just be a "skin job"—the packaging of allowable bulk. There should be a concept for overall form. Here, at the top, six floors are cut away to soften the profile from the street. And at the bottom six floors are cut away, opening to a pocket park with a waterfall and shade trees.

1979
Louis Sullivan Award for Architecture
Tucker Award for the Sarah Scaife Gallery, Building Stone Institute
Hutchinson Medal, Chicago Horticultural Society
Eliot Noyes Critic, Harvard University Graduate School of Design
Municipal Art Society Award for Conservatory Restoration, N.Y. Botanical Garden
"Transformations in Modern Architecture," Museum of Modern Art

Crocker Art Museum Master Plan
Sacramento, California
Hildegarde Bergeim, Michael Timchula, Daniel Casey, Assocs.; Rosekrans and Broder; Carissimi Rohrer Assoc., Associate Architects
The Crocker Mansion and Art Gallery date from the 1870s. A square service block with gallery above was added in 1969. In 1979 we designed a pavilion (with elevator) linking the two original buildings. In 1993 we completed master plans for a new three-story wing with top-lit galleries connected to the mansion by a third-floor bridge. This will create full circulation around the court through a chain of galleries.

1980
AIA Firm Award

Chairman's Certificate for Excellence in the Restoration of the N.Y. Botanical Garden, New York Landmarks Conservancy

Honor Award for the Yale University School of Organization and Management, Connecticut Society of Architects

Honorary Trustee, Haystack Mountain School of Crafts

Thomas Jefferson Professor in Architecture, University of Virginia

Georgia Museum of Art
Athens, Georgia, Project
Hildegarde Bergeim, Assoc.
Sited on a hill overlooking the campus, this museum suggests an acropolis. A block of exhibition galleries forms a podium. On top are separate structures: office pavilion, lecture hall, pyramidal skylight over central court, and monumental gateway. The approach is from a broad stepped ramp or over a bridge from the campus.

Housing
University of Virginia, Charlottesville, 1984
Thomas Czarnowski, Assoc.; Robert Junk, Proj. Arch.
At Alderman and Stadium Roads, on the campus outskirts, a great ring of student housing steps up and down around a woodland bowl. Outside walkways serve duplex suites.

House in Dallas
Dallas, Texas, 1983
Armand Avakian Associates, Associate Architects

See page 54

1981
Thomas Jefferson Medal in Architecture, University of Virginia

599 Lexington Avenue
New York, New York, 1986
John Lee, Partner; Robert Segal, Siglinde Stern, Richard Ridge, Proj. Archs.; Gajinder Singh, Proj. Arch., Subway Concourse

See page 166

Old Stone Square
Providence, Rhode Island, 1985
John Lee, Partner; Michael Timchula, Assoc.; Amelie Rennolds, Proj. Arch.
The building is designed on a cubic module: the floor-to-floor and column-grid dimensions are both divisible by four feet, eight inches. Stone facings, windows, porch, roof setbacks—indeed all facade details—are true squares. The material is polished and thermal gray granite with gray glass.

Equitable Tower West
New York, New York, 1986
Percy Keck, Partner; Steven Fisher,
David Wallance, Proj. Archs.; Lien Chen
A 1.6-million-square-foot, 51-story
tower. The major amenities are an
atrium, galleries, grand hallways, an
arcade, auditorium, pool, rooftop dining
rooms, and commissioned art. The
building was redesigned many times.
Compare early and final designs at right
and far right.

Mathematics and Computer Science Building
Amherst College, Massachusetts 1984
John Lee, Partner; Henry Myerberg,
Proj. Arch.
A contextual design for an old campus.
The computer laboratories and
classrooms are in a low horizontal wing;
the faculty offices and library, in a
tower.

1982
"New American Museum Architecture,"
Whitney Museum of American Art

Award of Honor for Art and Culture,
Mayor of the City of New York

Condominiums
Palm Beach, Florida, 1986
John Lee, Partner; Thomas Czarnowski,
Assoc.
Condominium apartments on the ocean
with arches, towers, and porches in the
spirit of older resorts. The entrance and
parking are completely below grade so
that there may be ground-floor
apartments.

Schine Student Center
Syracuse University, New York, 1986
Alistair Bevington, Partner; James
Wong, Proj. Arch.
A pinwheel plan sited on a hillside.
Union, bookstore, concert hall, and
student center rotate around a skylit
court. Brick "streets" lead in from four
directions. The building is orange brick,
and the main floor is expressed as a
black-glass and glazed-brick stripe.

1983
Honor Award for the Museum of Fine
Arts Addition and Remodeling, New
Mexico Society of Architects

Honorary Doctor of Fine Arts, Rhode
Island School of Design

Mehta House
Islesboro, Maine, 1985, 1993
Henry Myerberg, Proj. Arch., 1985
David Wallance, Proj. Arch., 1993
A four-story family house on rugged land
looking down to the sea. Later we added
an asymmetrical wing on a half level.
Ved Mehta wanted no concessions made
for his blindness.

1984
Honorary Doctor of Humane Letters,
Amherst College

Excellence in Design Awards for IBM
590 Madison Avenue and the Dallas
Museum of Art, New York State
Association of Architects

Advisory Council, Trust for Public Land
(until 1991)

Katonah Museum of Art
Katonah, New York, 1990
John Barnes, Proj. Arch.
An intimate museum for traveling
exhibits. A central hall, with square
galleries on each side, leads through the
building. Ahead is the sculpture garden,
framed by a low wall and shaded by
towering Norway spruces. Offices are
upstairs under sloping roofs with big
skylights. A tipped square window lights
the stairs.

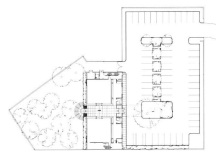

1984

Dormitories
Middlebury College, Vermont, 1986
John Lee, Partner; Daniel Hoffman,
Proj. Arch.
This chain of dormitories runs downhill
for a total of five floors, never more than
three stories in any one block, with
continuous hipped roofs. The materials
are contextual: gray limestone with a
lead-coated copper roof.

Computer Center
Bryn Mawr College, Pennsylvania, 1986
Henry Myerberg, Proj. Arch.

See page 108

1985

Tucker Award for the Dallas Museum of
Art, Building Stone Institute

Albert S. Bard Award for Excellence in
Architecture and Urban Design for the
IBM 590 Madison Avenue Plaza
Garden, City Club of New York

Allen Library
University of Washington, Seattle, 1991
Daniel Casey, Assoc.; Michael Barratt,
Proj. Arch.

See page 114

1986

First Award for Design Excellence for
Amherst College Mathematics and
Computer Science Building,
International Masonry Institute, New
England Chapter

Sidney L. Strauss Award, New York
Society of Architects

AIA Honor Award for House in Dallas

350th Anniversary Medal, Harvard
University

Minneapolis Sculpture Garden
Minneapolis, Minnesota, 1988
Alistair Bevington, Partner

See page 206

StoneCrest
San Diego, California
John Lee, Partner; Tucker, Sadler & Associates, Associate Architects
Master Plan, 1990
Michael Timchula, Assoc.; Michael Barratt, Proj. Arch.
Phase I, 1991
David Wallance, Proj. Arch.
An ambitious twenty-year, three-hundred-acre research and development park
including hotel, retail, and office facilities (four million square feet) with a new
freeway interchange and trolley connections. Four bold, eye-shaped terraces step
down the hill. The first terrace, with green-glass circular office towers, has been
completed and rented.

Dormitories
Deerfield Academy, Deerfield,
Massachusetts, 1989
Daniel Casey, Assoc.; Timothy Waters,
Proj. Arch.
New dormitories are interspersed
between old dormitories and a dining
hall. The scale, cornice lines, window
rhythms, brick color, and roof planes all
respect the past. The result is a quiet,
strong new campus quadrangle.

Hulman Pavilion,
Indianapolis Museum of Art
Indianapolis, Indiana, 1990
James Wong, Richard Klibschon, Proj.
Archs.
The Hulman Pavilion balances an older
auditorium across the entrance plaza. A
new chain of galleries creates
continuous circulation with splashes of
daylight from skylights and windows.
Separate galleries house temporary
exhibitions and a special collection.

Knoxville Museum of Art
Knoxville, Tennessee, 1989
Benjamin Kracauer, Proj. Arch.
Built on a hillside. From the entrance one ascends to quiet, top-lit galleries or descends to a spacious multipurpose room opening out to sculpture gardens with adjacent bookstore, orientation room, café, and auditorium. It really is a museum over a community center. The material is pink Tennessee marble.

1987
"Edward Larrabee Barnes Museum Designs," The Katonah Gallery

The Hyde Collection Addition
Glens Falls, New York, 1989
Alistair Bevington, Partner; John Barnes, Proj. Arch.
The Hyde Collection consisted of two houses. Our plan links them together. The new pavilion provides a central entrance and a large gallery for temporary exhibits and unifies the complex. A monumental stair leads down to an auditorium.

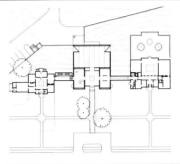

Armand Hammer Museum of Art and Cultural Center
Los Angeles, California, 1990
Daniel Casey, Assoc.; David Wallance, Proj. Arch.; Gruen Assocs., Associate Architects
Hammer dominated the creation of this cultural center behind his company headquarters. An arcade, galleries, auditorium, and library surround a courtyard which has an archway looking out to the city. The material is gray and white marble.

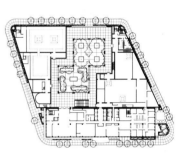

Birmingham Museum of Art
Expansion, Renovation, and Sculpture Garden
Birmingham, Alabama, 1993
Anne Wattenberg, Proj. Arch.; Sculpture Garden with Elyn Zimmerman; Kidd/Plosser/Sprague/Architects/Inc., Associate Architects
The new wing projects from the old museum, with a sweeping glass stair hall leading up from a lower entrance past auditorium, café, and bookstore to top-level galleries. Outside, a terraced sculpture garden steps up from a tree-shaded tile pavement to an upper terrace framed by a pergola, trees, and a bold rock waterwall.

1988

125 West Fifty-fifth Street
New York, New York, 1989
John Lee, Percy Keck, Partners; Steven Fisher, Assoc.
Sited next to the landmarked City Center on a dense urban block, this office building provides a through-block hallway to a south-facing plaza. Mirrored green glass makes the facades illusory.

Thurgood Marshall Federal Judiciary Building
Washington, D.C., 1992
John Lee, Partner; Michael Barratt, Proj. Arch.; J. Todd Achelpohl

See page 174

David Rockefeller House
Livingston, New York, 1990
Zehra Kuz, Amelie Rennolds, Proj. Archs.

1988

Royal Pines Resort
Queensland, Australia, 1991
John Lee, Partner; Siglinde Stern, Proj. Arch.; Media Five Assoc., Associate Architects
A resort hotel and conference center surrounded by a twenty-seven-hole golf course. Instead of the usual rectangle or square, this plan is a triangle. The form opens wide to surrounding views yet seems illusory from the golf course. At ground level the angles generate land and water forms that pinwheel outward.

Computer Center
University of California, Berkeley, 1994
John Barnes, Mark Cavagnero, Proj. Archs.; Anshen + Allen, Associate Architects
Five floors: lecture- and classrooms at the bottom, faculty offices at the top. A strong facade faces the campus, reinforcing the street wall. To the rear, the mass steps back with garden terraces on each level. The material is glazed olive-green tile.

1989
Honor Award for Sweeney Chapel, Christian Theological Seminary, Interfaith Forum on Religion, Art, and Architecture

"Federal Judiciary Office Building Competition," National Building Museum

Fine Arts Museums of San Francisco
Daniel Casey, Assoc.; Barnes and Cávagnero, Associate Architects
Master Plan, M. H. de Young Memorial Museum, 1990
California Palace of the Legion of Honor Renovation and Expansion, 1995
David Wallance, Proj. Arch.
Our work began in 1989 with a master plan for the M. H. de Young Memorial Museum. The first phase of the project is the renovation and expansion of the historic California Palace of the Legion of Honor. Below the Court of Honor we have designed a new gallery floor with a low pyramidal skylight. A new service entrance, storage areas, and support facilities occupy the level below.

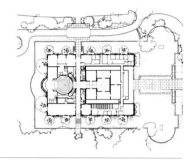

National University of Singapore
John Lee, Partner; Daniel Casey, Assoc.; Indeco, Associate Architects
Master Plan, 1991; Fine Arts Complex, Project; Kentvale Faculty and Staff Housing, 1995
Our master plan proposes a new ring-road system with massing and siting for new buildings. For the first phase, faculty and staff apartments step up the hill across from the main entrance.

Southwestern Medical Center
University of Texas, Dallas, 1993, 1995
John Lee, Partner; Steven Fisher, Assoc.; F&S Partners; OmniPlan Inc., Associate Architects
The Phase I and II towers are the first in a chain of diagonally connected research buildings planned for the North Campus. While these and future towers will be separate, horizontal circulation will be possible. The entire project will take twenty years.

Unitarian Universalist Society
Manhasset, New York, 1993
Percy Keck, Partner; Amelie Rennolds, Richard Ridge, Proj. Archs.
On a wooded site next to an old stone mansion, the complex includes a worship hall with school, children's chapel, tower, multipurpose room, gallery, offices, and more. The materials are granite fieldstone, wood walls and ceilings, and colored glass in two planes by James Carpenter.

Connecticut Tennis Center

Yale University, New Haven, Connecticut, 1991
John Lee, Partner; Daniel Casey, Assoc.; Richard Klibschon, Joseph Weiss, Proj. Archs.
Built into woods on a hillside, this stadium has its entrance halfway up the stands, where there is an ambulatory walk. Seating opens out symmetrically on all sides. The material is precast concrete. The stadium design *and* construction took only eleven months.

1990

First Honor Award for IBM World Trade Corporation, AIA Westchester/ Mid-Hudson Chapter

1991

Member, American Academy of Arts and Letters

1992

Outstanding Tennis Facility Award for the Connecticut Tennis Center, United States Tennis Association

Dorothy Schmidt Center

Florida Atlantic University, Boca Raton, 1994
John Lee, Partner; Charles Perry, Proj. Arch.; Schwab, Twitty and Hanser, Associate Architects
An arts center around a great sloping lawn shaped for outdoor performances. To the west is an existing concert hall; to the south, a performing arts building; to the north, a humanities building; and to the east, art studios overlooking a pond.

Mann Library Expansion

Cornell University, New York, 1998
Percy Keck, John Lee, Partners; Steven Fisher, Assoc.
Mann Library is an internationally recognized reference center. This multiphased project will be built over many years. Phase I, the library addition, will be completed in 1998. In subsequent phases the library will be renovated and a hortorium added.

1993

Life Trustee, Museum of Modern Art

Alumni Lifetime Achievement Award, Harvard University Graduate School of Design

Brick in Architecture Award for the Allen Library, University of Washington, AIA/Brick Institute of America

1994

AIA Twenty-Five-Year Award for Haystack Mountain School of Crafts

Partners, Associates, and Staff

Lisa Abrams
J. Todd Achelpohl
Kathy Achelpohl
David Adler
James Aftreth
Owren Aftreth
Vijay Aggarwal
Claude Aldrich
Jacob Allderdicc
Herbert Alicandri
Jay Alpert
Albert Amerson
Robert Andersen
William Andersen
David Arnold
Ellen Aronsohn
Frederic Ashworth
Bernard Askienazy
Armand Avakian
Arthur Baker
Richard Balser
Ward Bancroft
Cynthia Banzon
John Barnes
Mary Barnes
Michael Barratt
Suanne Bassett
Bal Baswant
Gregory Bates
Kadambari Baxi
Bruce Becker
John Belbusti
Amy Benenson
Richard Berenholtz
Hildegarde Bergeim
Cara Berton
Sibel Bertuna
Ieva Berzins
Helen Best
Jean-Robert Betremieux
Alistair Bevington
Christopher Bickford
Robert Bier
Nancy Bissell
Bruce Blakeslee
John Bloom
Paul Boccuzza
Brigid Boltman
Ann Borst
Rufus Bostow
Robert Boucheron
Fernando Bracer
Richard Bradley
Daniel Brown
Hillary Brown
Al Brownell
Cormac Buggy
Niamh Butler
David Cagle
Irving Cahn
William Cahoon

Perez Cantrell
Martha Carder
Stephen Carter
Daniel Casey
Richard Caust
Mark Cavagnero
William Cavellini
Judith Chafee
Tanya Chamberlain
Keith Champagne
Steven Chan
Shiao-Ling Chang
Steven Chang
Vincent Chang
Frank Chapman
Ayla Chatfield
David Chau
Casey Chen
Lien Chen
Linna Cheng
Ivan Chermayeff
Paula Cheung
Susan Chisholm
John Choi
Raveevarn Choksombatchai
Robin Cika
Marian Citroen
Roger Clarke
Nancy Coan
Louise Coccetti
Laura Cohen
Robert Cohen
Stuart Cohen
William Cohen
Constance Colosa
Joseph Colosa
Christopher Compton
Ponnamma Concessao
Robert Condon
Alexander Cooper, Jr.
Timothy Cooper
John Copelin
Nathan Corser
Frances Crabb
Karen Cronin
Sean Cryan
Thomas Czarnowski
Annette Daly
Maire Darby
Donald Davidson
Anna De Georgio
Joanne De Joy
Ward D'Elia
Joseph De Losa
Dickson De Marche
Bobbie De Souza
Michael Deskey
Eugenie Devine
Sidney Dombroff
Thomas Dryer
James Duffy

Patrice Dworzan
Ada Egeberg
Desmond Emanuel
Harry Eng
Linn Ericson
Jonathan Esman
Hobert Fairbank
Debra Fellion
Earl Ferguson
Ian Ferguson
Jennifer Fier
Nicholas Figliola
Ann Fishbein
Marie Fisher
Steven Fisher
Edward Fitzgerald
Patricia Flanagan
Richard Fletcher
Herman Flugman
John Fondrisi
Charles Forberg
Gregory Forfar
Christine Forrer
William Forster
Bruce Fowle
James Fraerman
Eugene Futterman
Nancy Geng
Edward Georges
James Gettinger
Stephen Giannelli
Sidney Gilbert
William Gillespie
Russell Gilroy
Herbert Goldberg
Rose Goldenson
Martin Golder
Ira Goldfarb
Thomas Goldfrank
Daniel Goldner
Luanne Goodson
Steven Gorbea
Jack Gordon
Roseanne Gordon
Matthew Gottsegen
Robert Gough
Worth Graham
Warren Gran
Robert Gray
Susan Green
Thomas Guerin
Charles Gwathmey
William Haasters
Deborah Haffly
Victoria Hage
John Hagmann
Emmett Hagood
Kendall Hamman
Kate Hanenberg
Jeffrey Harrigan
Melissa Harris

Susan Harris
Robert Hart
Roy Haskell
Margaret Haworth
Ian Hayes
Marion Haynes
Arthur Helbock
Laura Heller
Christopher Hemphill
Albert Henriques
Linda Herd
Carlos Heredia
Martin Hero
Eta Herschman
Kar-Hwa Ho
William Hodgson
Daniel Hoffman
Nigel Honer
John Hordyk
Masahiro Horiuchi
James Horizny
Herbert Howley
Charles Hoyt
Lillian Hsu
Sandra Huang
Kenneth Hughee
Kazunari Ide
Gerald Ilowite
Martin Inwood
Mitzi Irizarry
Edward Jacobson
Jonathan Jaffe
Ajyzk Jagoda
Janet Jakubowski
Fritz Jeanty
Everardo Jefferson
Archibald Johnson
Charles Johnson
Robert Junk
Irving Kahn
Lubomyr Kalynycz
Addison Kantor
Steven Kaplan
Lisa Kapp
Beyhan Karahan
Rolf Karl
Alexander Kasuba
Percy Keck
Trevor Keetley
Arthur Kegerris
Edward Kelbish
Richard Keller
E. Lee Kennedy
Patrick Kennedy
Stephen Kerpen
George Kewin
Dorothee King
Kwang-Yu King
Steven King
Eleanor Klein
Judy Klein

Richard Klibschon
Roni Kopels
Lester Korzilius
Benjamin Kracauer
Pieter Kramer
Marianne Kugler
Cesarae Kukulski
Zehra Kuz
Everett La Coss
Paul Laird
Justin Lamb
Eric Landers
Daniel Lanni
George Large
Eugene Lau
Harry Lau
Marie Lawrence
Norman Lebowitz
Yann Lecoanet
Duk Won Lee
John M. Y. Lee
John V. Y. Lee
Paul Lee
Una Lee
William Lee
Joseph Lengeling
Heng-Choong Leong
Cynthia Levinson
Stanley Lewis
Gerald Li
Irene Li
Kevin Lichten
Paul Lochart
Ivor Loefing
Neil Logan
Donald London
Harry Lord
Jeremiah Low
John Lucas
Gregory Luhan
Irene Luhn
Arthur Lutzker
Jacqueline Lynfield
Virginia Lyon
Ching-Po Ma
Eugene Magenau
Hazel Manley
Sarah Manley
Doris Marachnick
Susan Martin
Anton Martinez
Joseph Matulewski
Stanley Maurer
June Maxwell
Edward Mazria
Linda McCall
Patrick McElwee
Olivia McLaren
Anthony McLeod
James McLeod
Philip McMahon

Martin McNeill
John Menz
Joseph Merz
Nancy Miao
Michelle Miceli
Frank Michel
Kristine Miller
Marshall Miller
Mary Ann Miller
Frank Miro
Marvin Mitchell
Beatrice Moger
Richard Moger
John Molloy
Peter Morgan
Toshiko Mori
Allen Mullins
Martin Munter
Henry Myerberg
Peter Mykytyn
Paul Nakazawa
Theodore Naos
Afzaal Nasiruddeen
Sally Nason
Alfred Nelson
Ralph Nelson
Herbert Newman
Blaine Nicholls
Michael Noble
Regina Nobles
Chinwe Nwaogu
Chibuike Ogbonna
Marita O'Hare
Laurie Olin
Sally Olowecki
Sonia Olowecki
Audrey Page
Giovanni Pasanella
Alphonse Patenaude
Paul Pelletier
Tammy Peluso
Charles Perry
Herbert Peschel
Andrew Pettit
Henry Pierre
Gregory Plaza
Bonnie Pleasant
Panchita Plummer
Boris Pogacnik
Michael Polak
Mildred Popkin
April Pottorff
Raymond Prevete
Irene Pujol
Daniel Quinn
Kathleen Quinn
Carlene Ramus
James Rappa
Robert Reach
Iris Regn
Charles Rendale

Amelie Rennolds
Martin Rich
Stanley Richardson
Richard Ridge
Anna Rinker
Mary Beth Rizzo
Jaquelin Robertson
Benjamin Robinson
Blair Robinson
Fred Rodriguez
Victor Rodriquez
Gus Rohrs
Frederick Romley
Rafael Rosado
Candace Rosen
William Rosenblum
Harvey Rothenberg
Jack Rybner
Barbara Sageser
John Salvador
Ellen Salz
Demetri Sarantitis
Michael Scandiffio
Gisela Schaefer
Maya Schali
Jill Schick
Arthur Schmitz
Evan Schwartz
Sandra Schwartz
Victor Schwartz
Robert Segal
Amy Seiler
Philip Seligson
Murray Sellman
Robin Sen
Sassoon Shahmoon
Mary Shalvey
Lucille Sharf
Robert Siegel
Robin Sika
Madlen Simon
Gajinder Singh
Sandra Small
Peter Smith
Ginny Smoake
George Snow
Gilbert Sorenson
Philip Sowers
Michael Starr
Joseph Stella
Frederick Stelle
Oona Stern
Siglinde Stern
William Stern
Eugene Steuben
Bernadette Stiga
Felicia Stimburis
Theodore Sulikowski
Daniel Sullivan
Carol Surico
Guy Szeto

Rachel Tanur
Tapani Tapanainen
Adina Taylor
Kokseng Teng
Clifford Thacher-Renshaw
Shirley Thomas
Elsie Thoy
Anne Tichich
David Tidey
Michael Timchula
Frank Tomaino
Joseph Tonetti
Diana Tredennick
Bruce Trewin
Renato Trotta
Jean-Pierre Varin
Pablo Vengoechea
Antanas Vytuvis
David Wallance
Claire Ward
Theresa Ward
Charles Wassa
Timothy Waters
Francis Watkins
Virginia Watler
Maria Watson
Anne Wattenberg
Sheldon Weber
William Weber
Muffy Webster
Kwang-Hsin Wei
Thomas Weigel
Irving Weiner
Richard Weinstein
Myles Weintraub
Joseph Weiss
John Whedbee
Antoinette White
Warren Winter
Peter Wirth
Ellen Wong
James Wong
Hoi Woo
Karen Wood
Robert Woodward
Loring Wou
Lowernton Wright
Stanley Wright
Mai-Tse Wu
Michael Wurmfeld
Takamori Yamazaki
Noel Yauch
Jack Yuan
Austin Zago
Dolores Zago
Ivan Zayac
Uiko Zecha
Fred Zeiger
Yong-Qin Zhang

Photo Credits

All numbers refer to page numbers.

Russ Adams Productions: 253 (Connecticut Tennis Center)
Robin Alexander: 247 (Duke University)
J. David Allison: 248 (Crocker Art Museum)
Gil Amiaga: 21, bottom
Bernard Askienazy: 152–53
Ken Balzer, photographer/Jeffrey Boyd, image composition:
212–13, middle
Edward L. Barnes: 62; 238 (WVIP Radio Station, left)
Daniel Barsotti: 220
Michael Baz 250: (Dormitories, Middlebury)
Craig Blackmon, AIA: 252 (Southwestern Medical Center)
Dick Brehl: 212, top
Steven Brooke: 246 (Museum of Art)
Mark Bunnell, Quennell Rothschild Associates: 206
(axonometric drawing)
Orlando Cabanban: 241 (W. D. Richards Elementary School)
Louis Checkman: 239 (Helen Newberry Joy Residence,
left); 240 (Freshman Dean's House); 241 (Wye Institute,
left); 242 (University of Chicago); 243 (Spring Hill); 249
(Equitable, right)
T. Whitney Cox: 248 (Housing)
George Cserna: 199; 240 (Administration Building); 241
(Wye Institute, right)
Steven Fisher: 252 (National University of Singapore)
Charles Forberg: 30–31
David Franzen/Esto: 48; 49; 50; 51; 52; 53; back cover
Jeff Goldberg/Esto: 174; 176–177; 178; 179; 180–181
Gorchev & Gorchev, Inc.: 144; 145
Ted Hansen: 247 (Utah State University)
Bob Harr, Hedrich-Blessing: 249 (Condominiums)
Jeffrey Harrigan: 246 (Indiana University, bottom)
Hedrich-Blessing: 148; 149
David Hirsch: 79; 81; 94–95; 237 (Fresh Air Fund Camps,
bottom left)
John Hollis: 228, top
William Hubbell: 237 (Barnes House)
Greg Hursley: 131; 246 (Indiana University, top)
Clemens Kalischer: 242 (Dormitories)
Barbara Karant: 130
Phokion Karas: 98–99
M. Lewis Kennedy, Jr.: 251 (Birmingham Museum of Art)
Balthazar Korab: 194; 195; 239 (Helen Newberry Joy
Residence, right)
Benjamin Kracauer: 251 (Knoxville Museum of Art)
N. Lieberman/T. Watts: 121
Thorney Lieberman: 244 (American Savings Bank); 248
(535 Madison Avenue)

Ulric Meisel: 236 (Weiner House)
Scott Miles: 249 (Katonah Museum of Art)
Marvin Mitchell: 119
Joseph W. Molitor: 74; 75; 84–85; 86; 87; 88–89; 92–93;
100–101; 102–103; 154–155; 156–157; 238 (WVIP Radio
Station, right); 241 (Andrew Rockefeller House)
Antonia Mulas: 24; 25; 26–27; 32; 33; 110; 111;
112–113; 124; 125; 126; 127; 128–129; 133; 136–137;
138; 139; 140 top; 141; 192–193; 196–197; 200–201;
202–203; 204–205; 207; 208–209; 218; 219; 221, bottom;
226, top; 228, bottom; 229; 230; 231; 232–233; 252
(Unitarian Universalist Society)
Jon Naar: 140, bottom
Lloyd Pearson: 238 (United States Consulate)
Gerald Ratto: 252 (Computer Center)
Louis Reens: 240 (Henry House)
Cervin Robinson: 160–161; 162; 163; 164; 165;
213, bottom
Steve Rosenthal: 77, middle left; 168; 169; 170; 171;
172–173; front cover
Ueli Roth: 38; 39, top
Steve Sartori: 249 (Schine Student Center)
Roberto Schezen: 216; 217; 221, top
Ben Schnall: 237 (Fresh Air Fund Camps, top;
Miller House)
Marshall L. Schultz: 242 (Student Union)
Julius Shulman, Hon. AIA: 17
Ezra Stoller/Esto: 22; 39, bottom; 40–41; 236 (Reid
House); 239 (Neiman Marcus); 242 (Guest House,
J. D. Rockefeller III); 243 (Rockefeller Hall)
Wes Thompson: 250 (StoneCrest)
Alexandra C. Timchula: 244 (Plants and Man Building);
245 (Museum of Pueblo and Navaho Art); 245 (Main Gate
and Conservatory Restoration); 249 (Equitable, left)
Robert Segal: 247 (1010 Market Street)
Siglinde Stern: 243 (St. Paul's School)
Brian Vanden Brink: 249 (Mehta House)
Francisco Vando: 21, top
John Veltri: 72–73; 76, middle right; 77, top right
Charles Walters: 245 (Music and Art Building)
Nick Wheeler: 56–57; 58; 59; 60–61; 64–65; 66–67;
68–69; 105; 107; 116–117; 184–185; 186; 187; 188–189;
224–225; 226, bottom; 227; 240 (Dormitories, left); 243
(Yale University, top); 247 (Asia Society); 248 (Old Stone
Square); 249 (Mathematics and Computer Science Building);
250 (Dormitories, Deerfield)
Takamori Yamazaki: 252 (Royal Pines Resort)